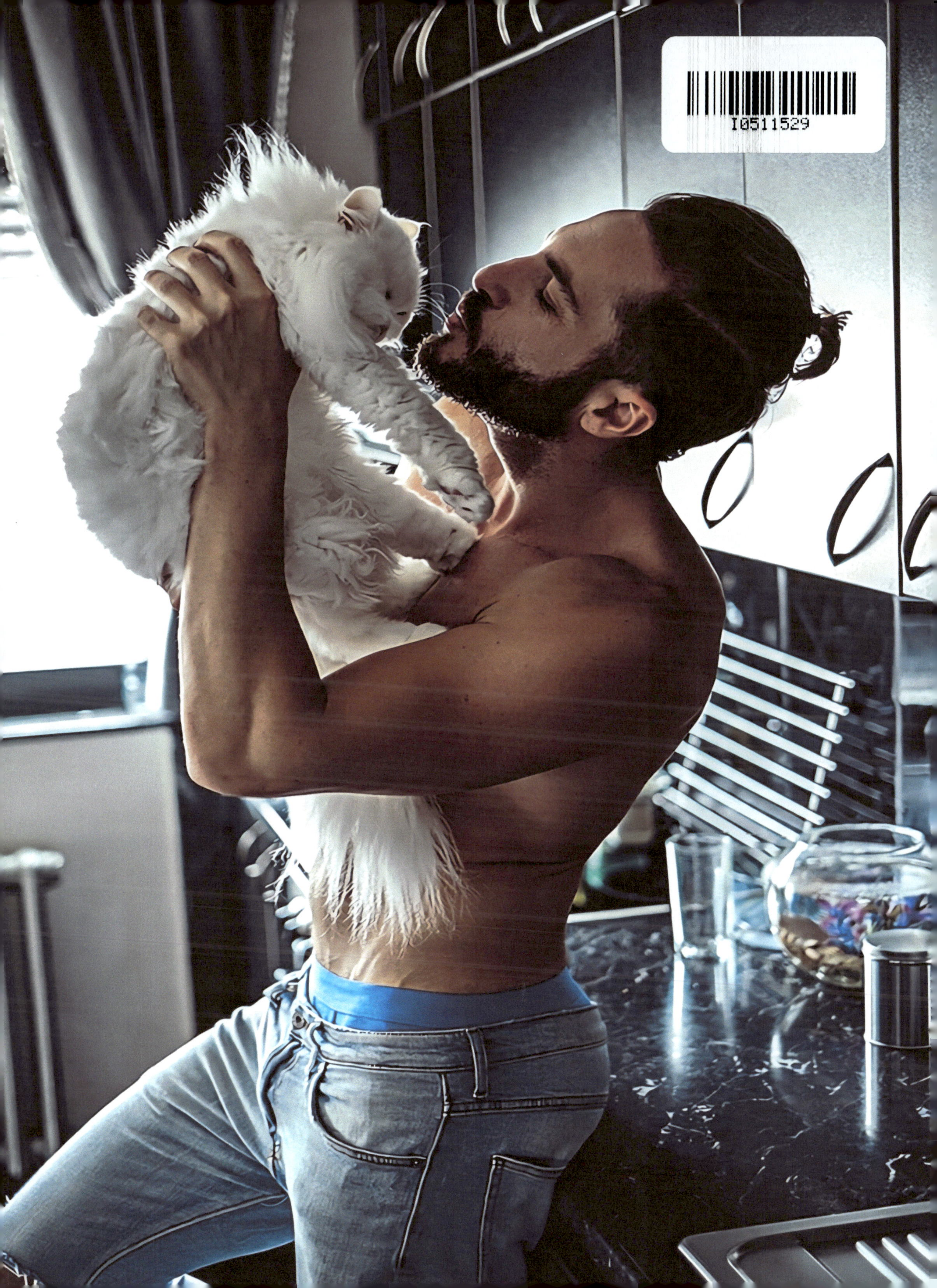

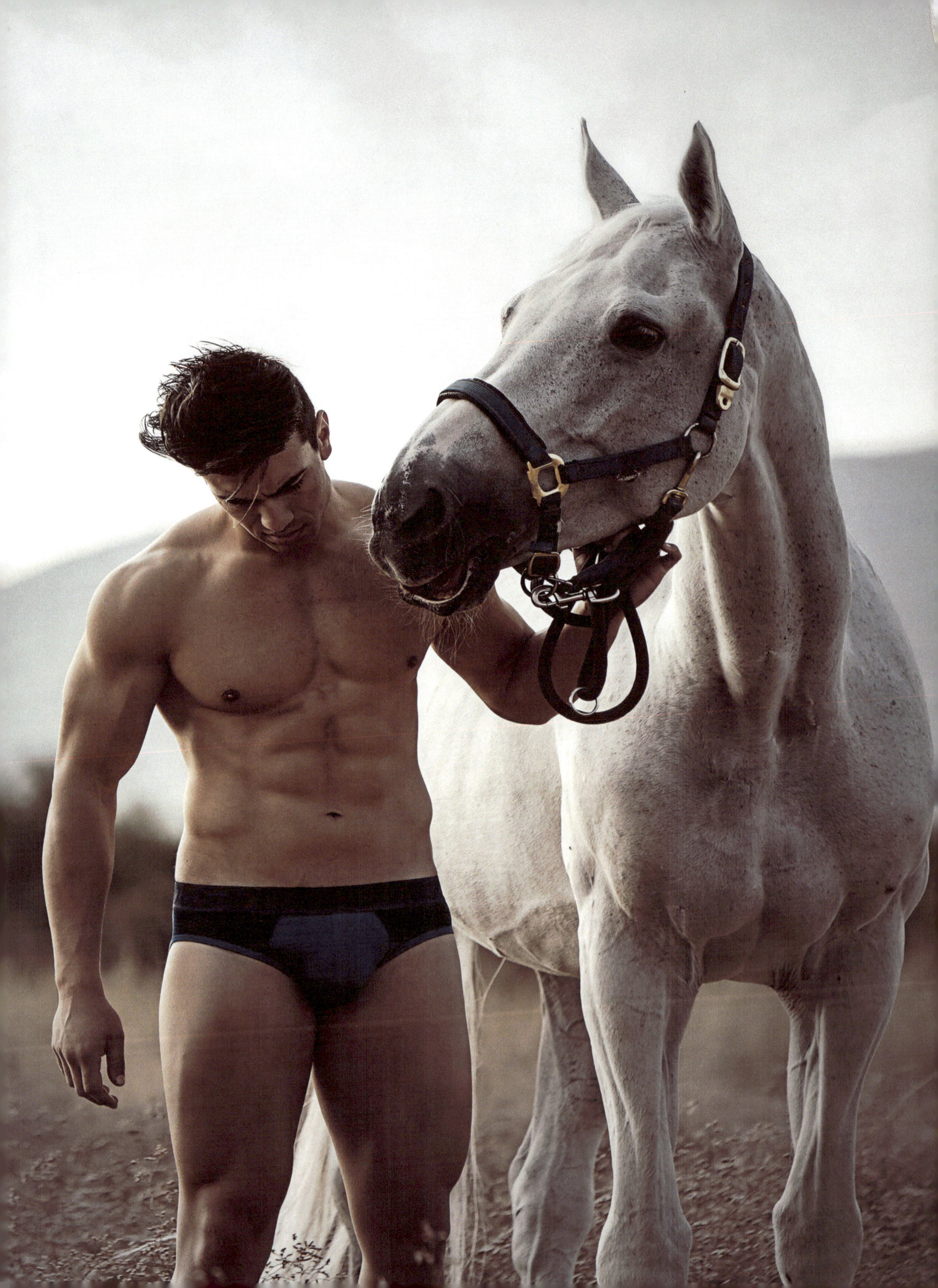

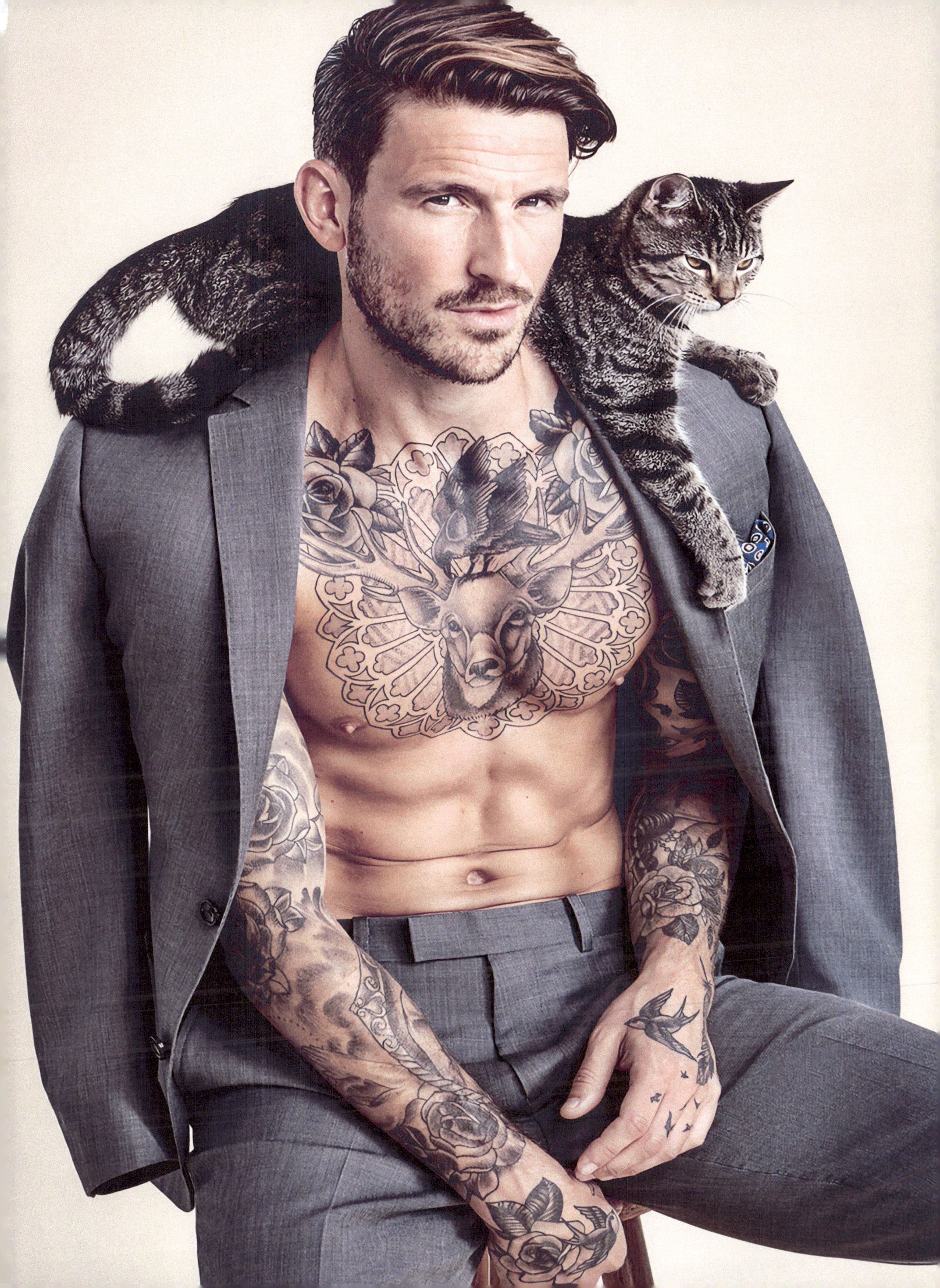

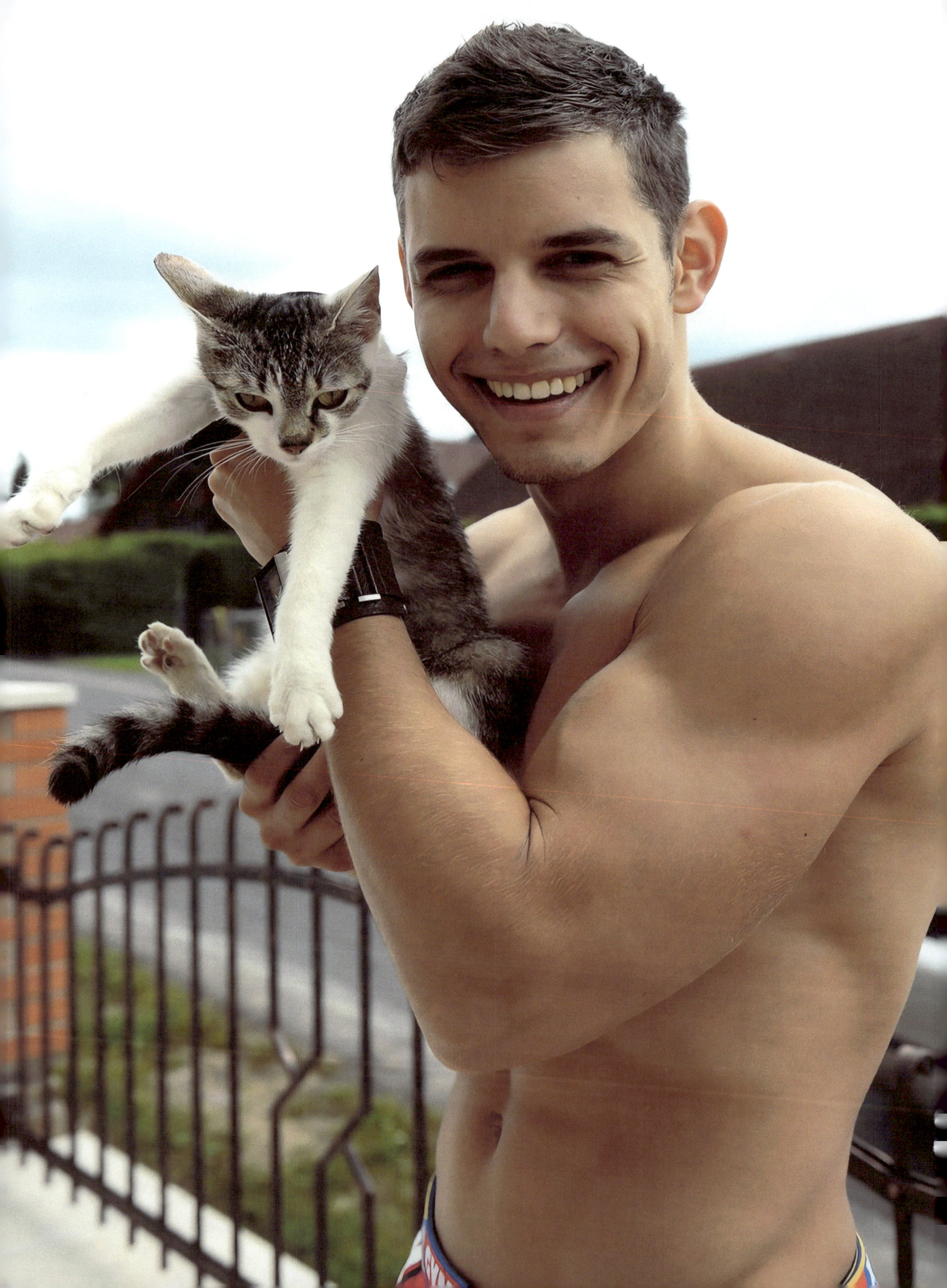

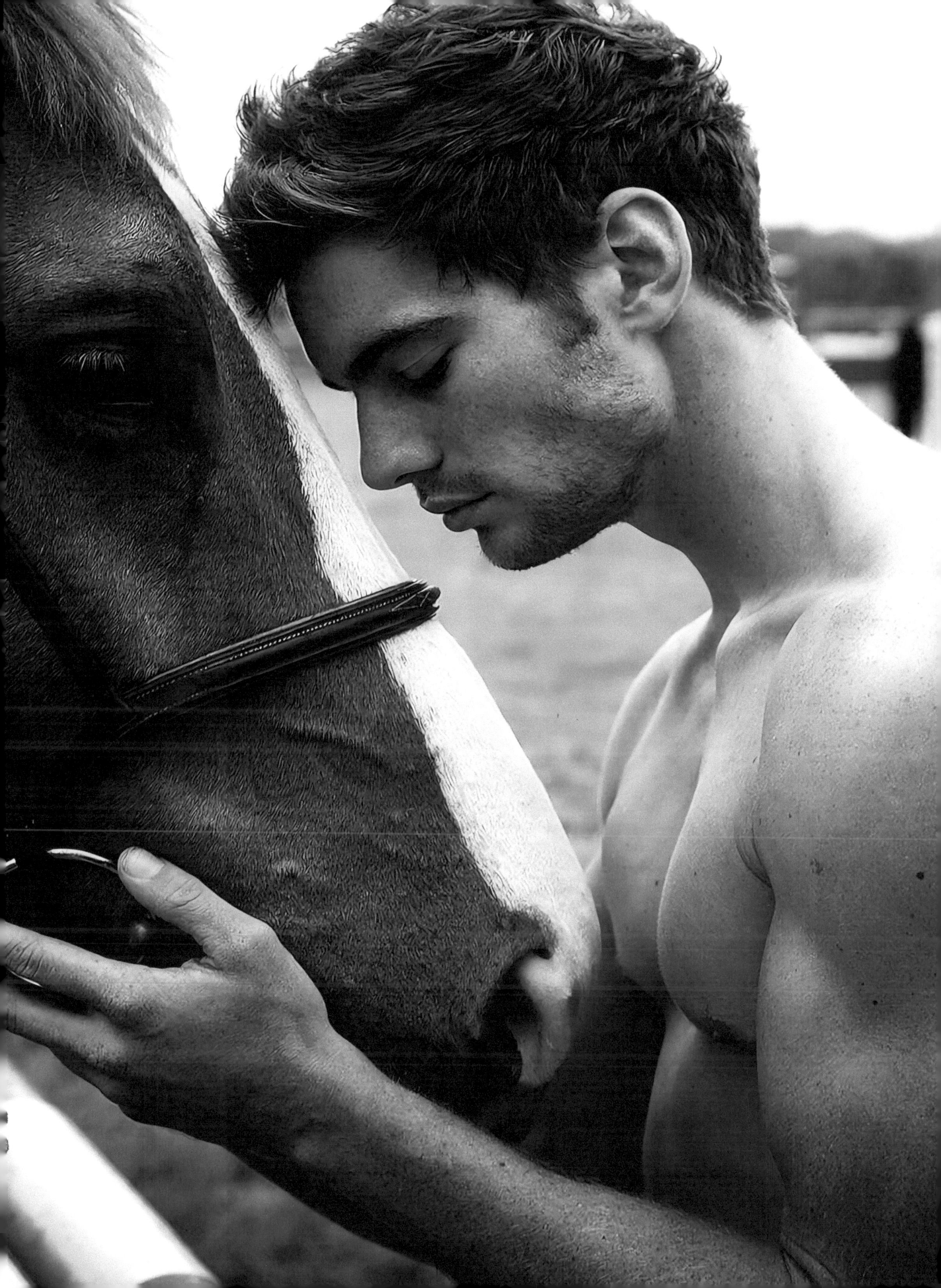

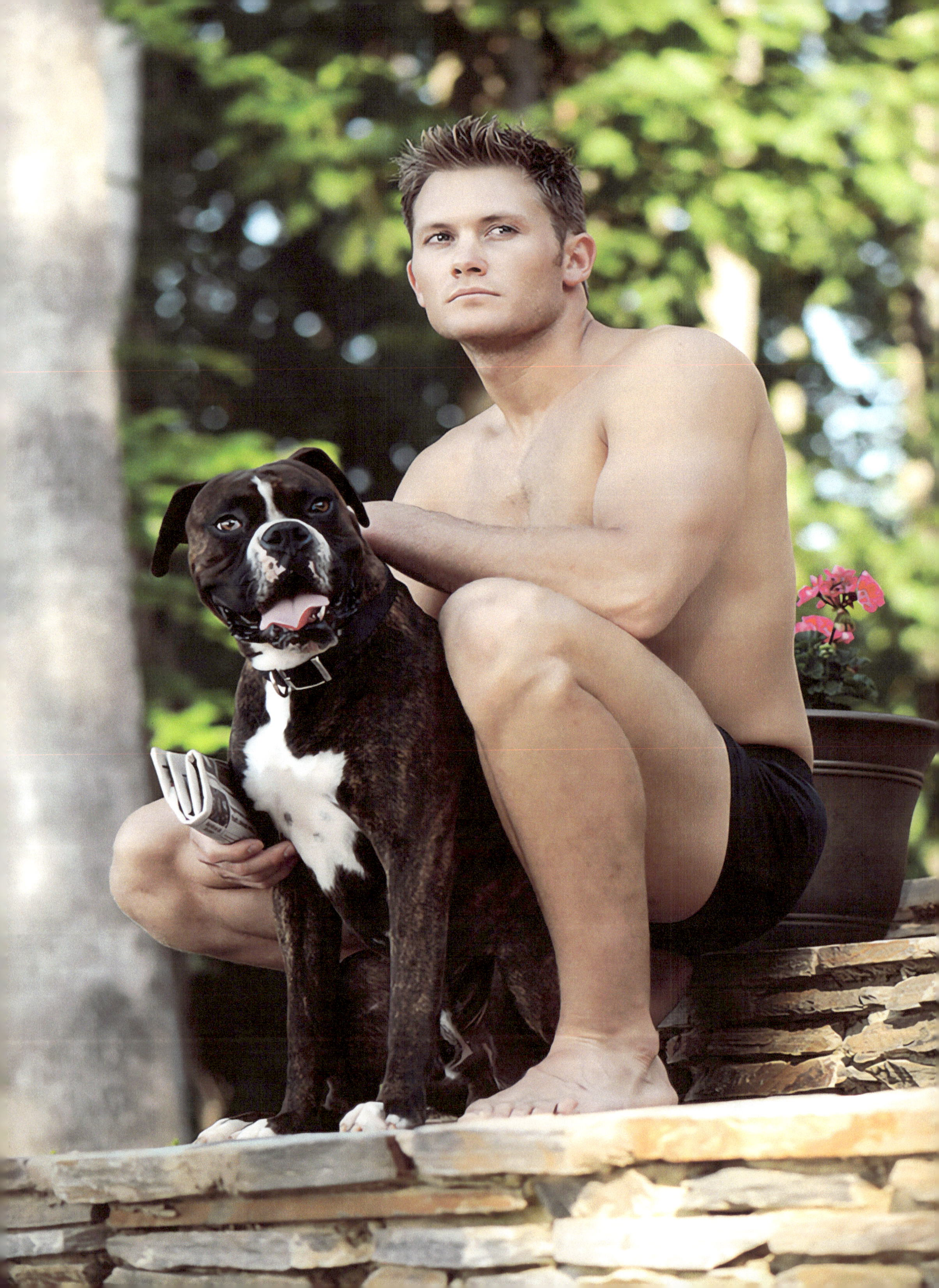

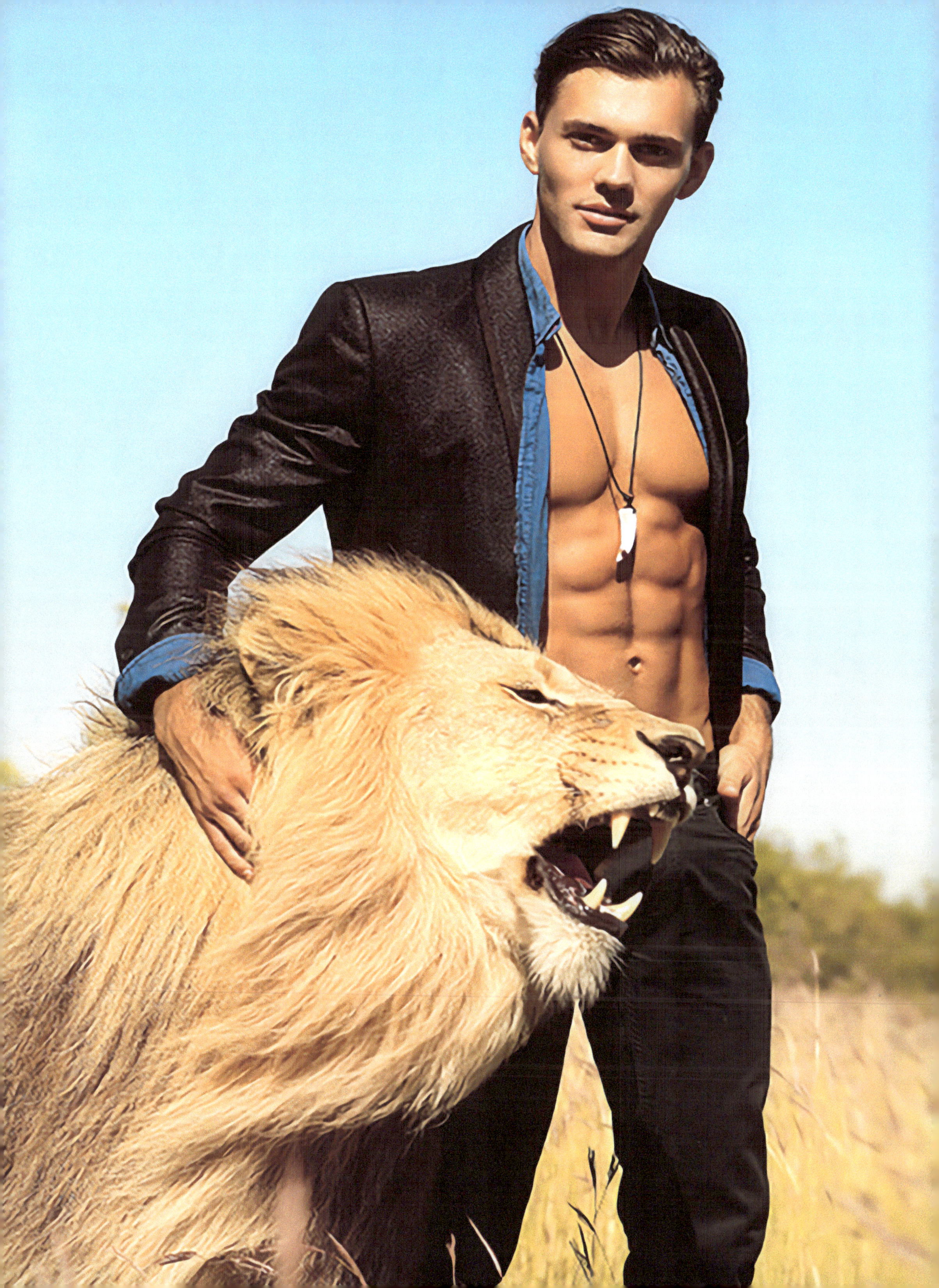

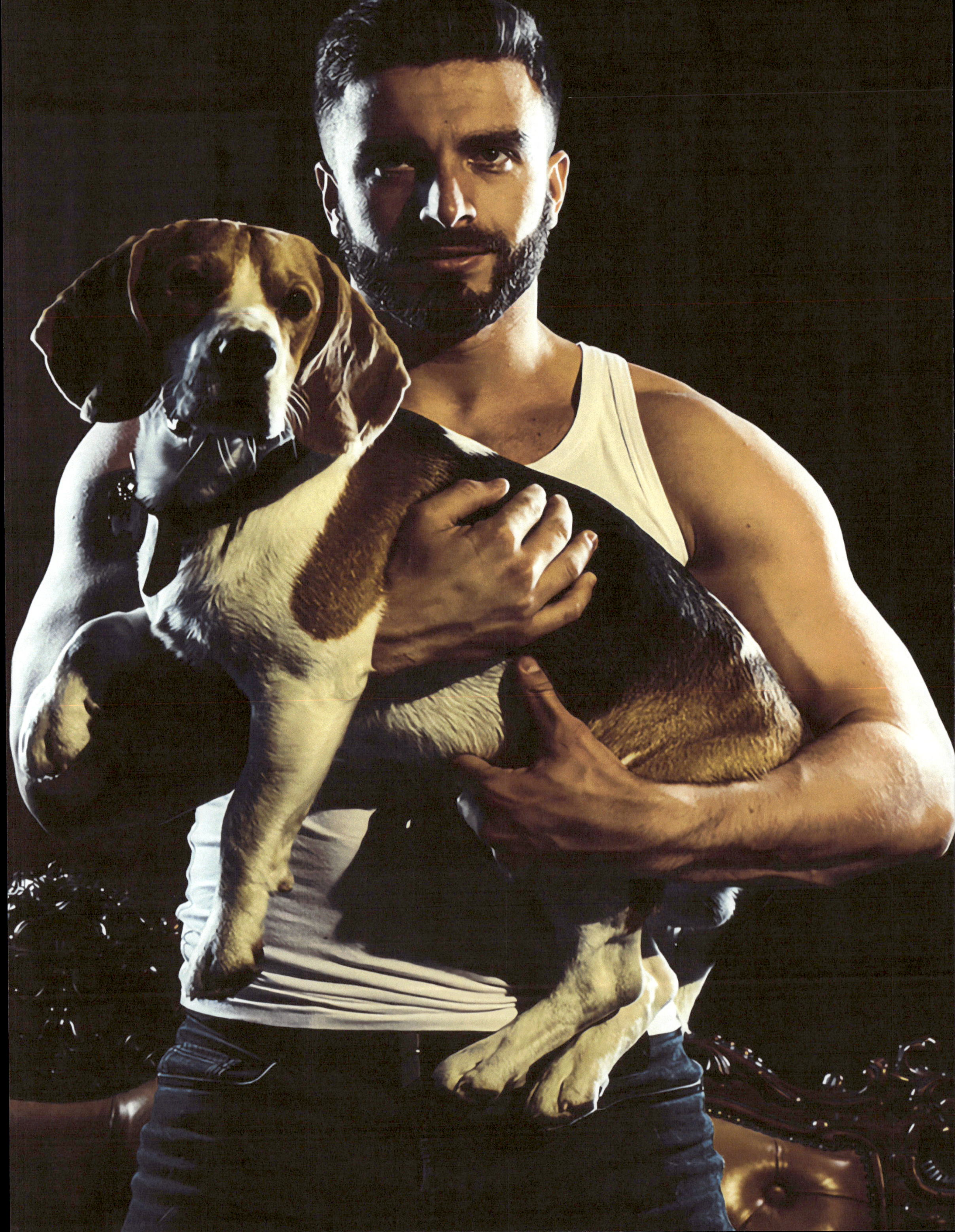

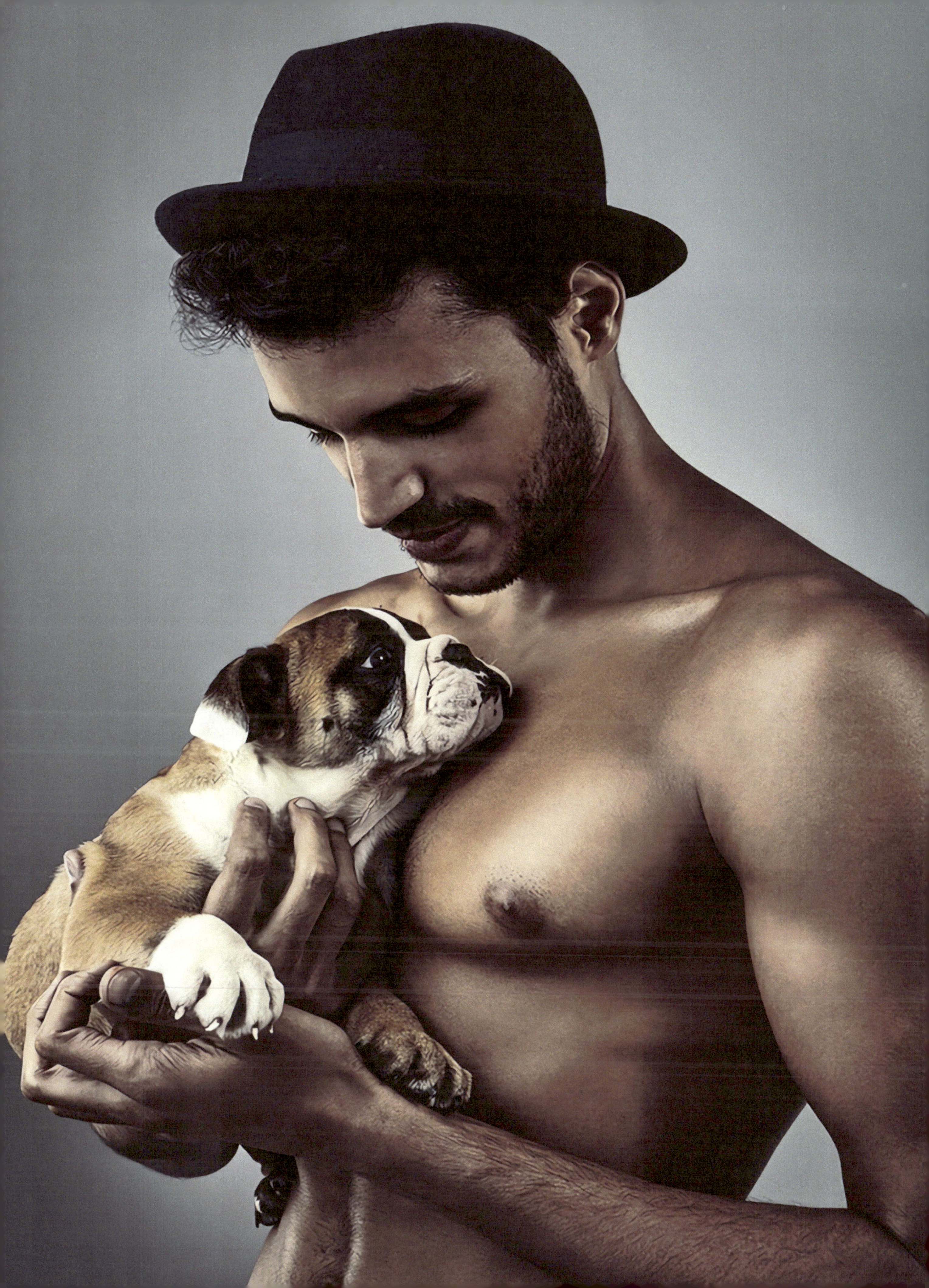

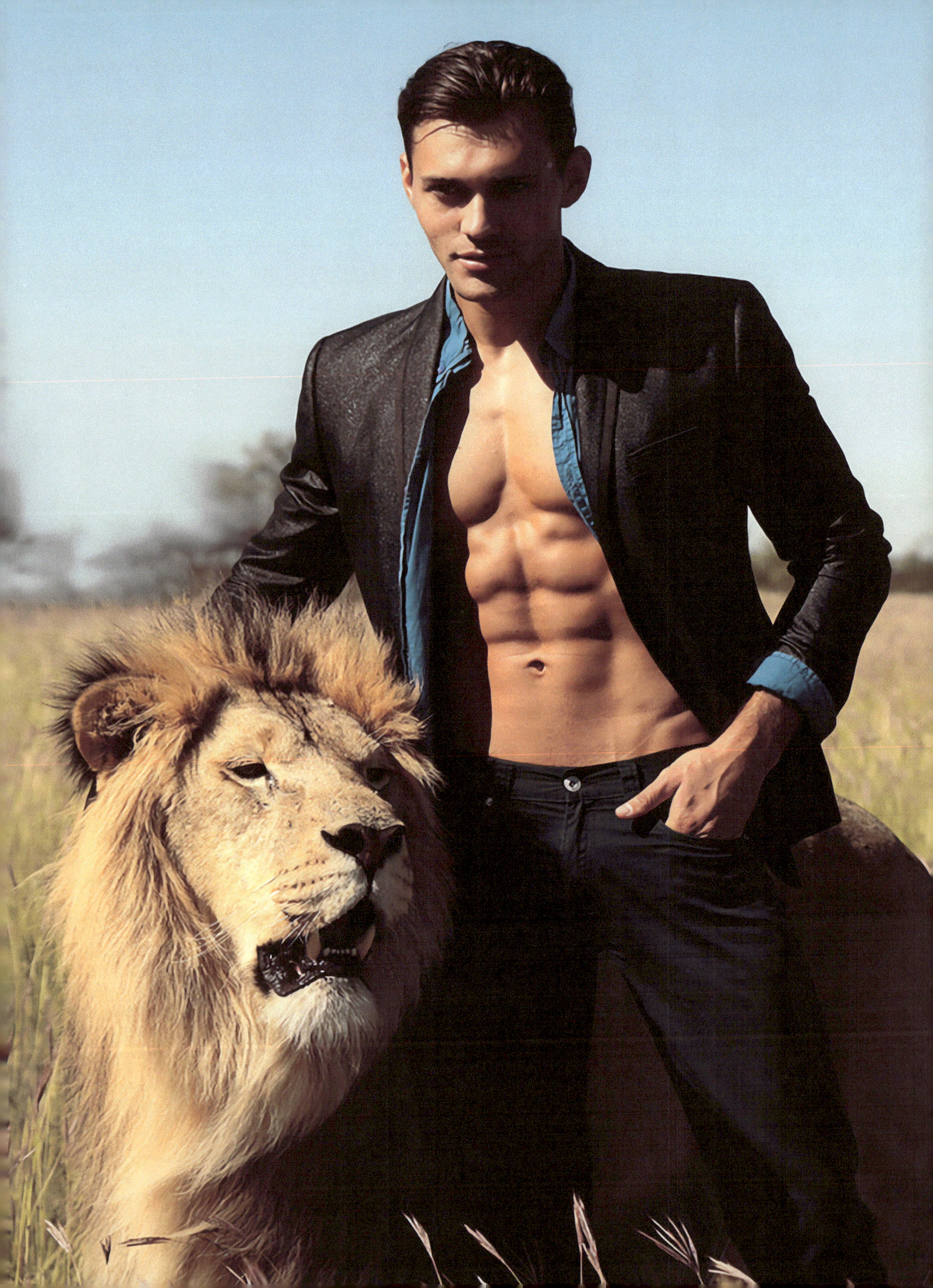

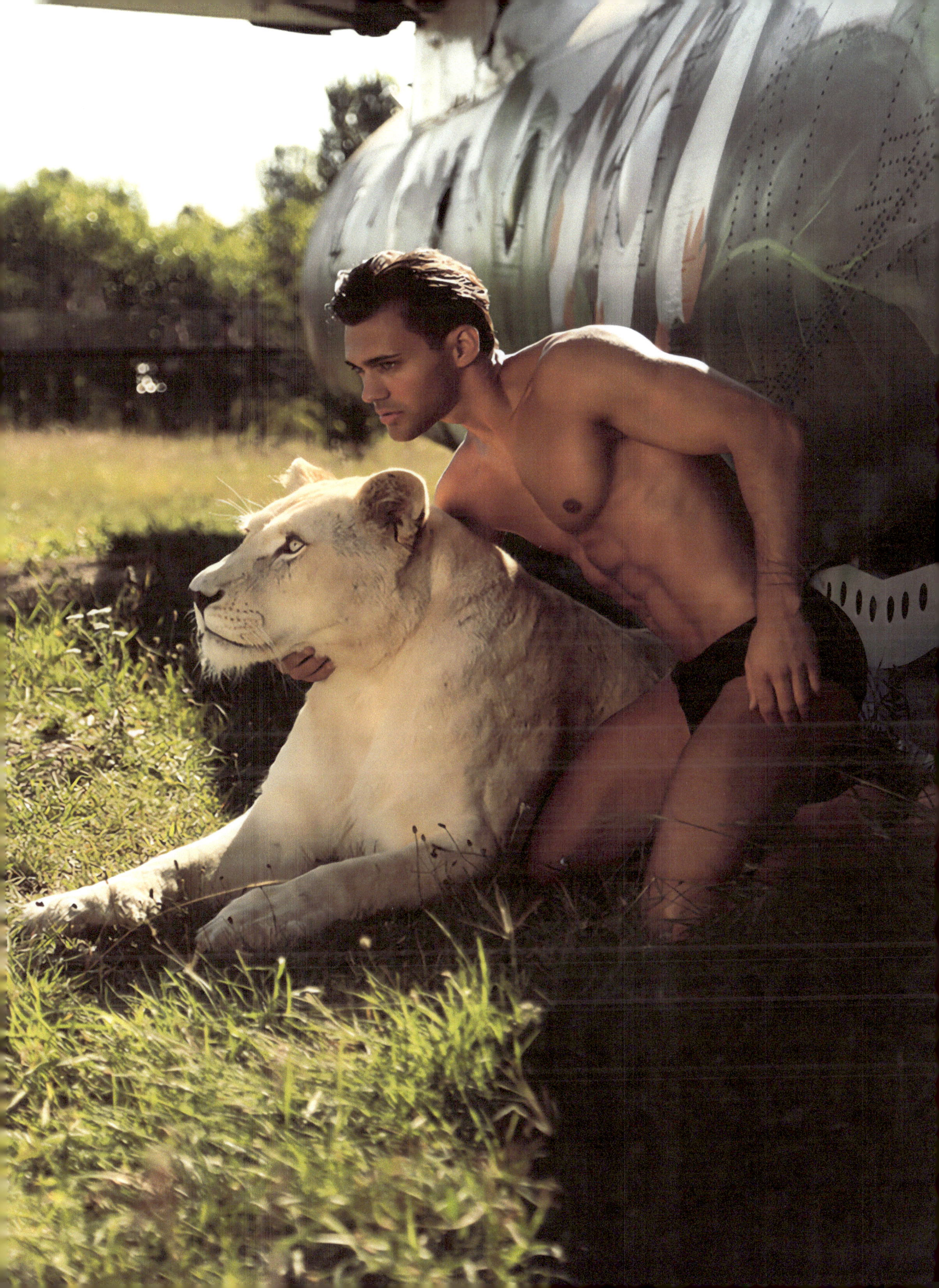

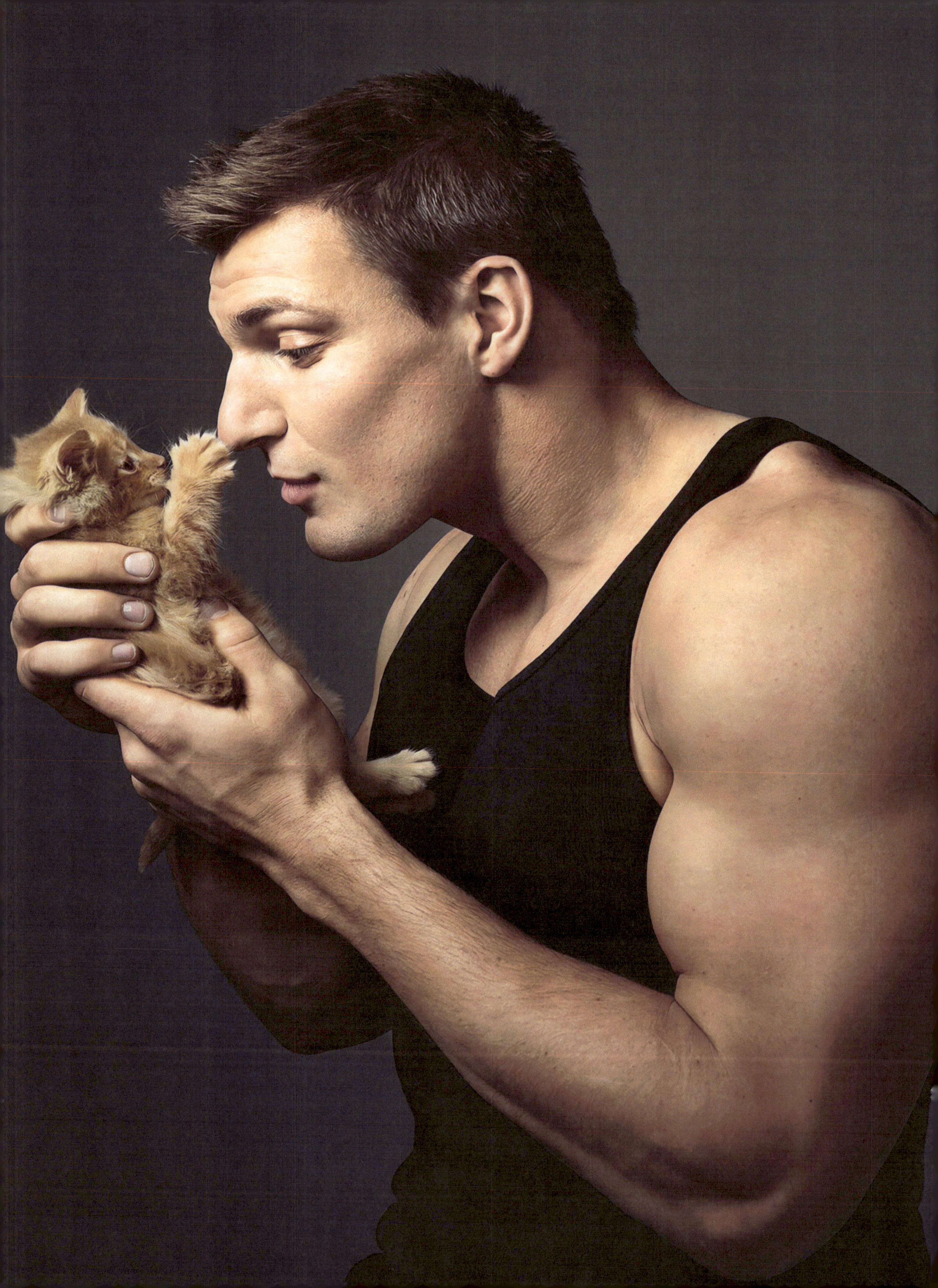

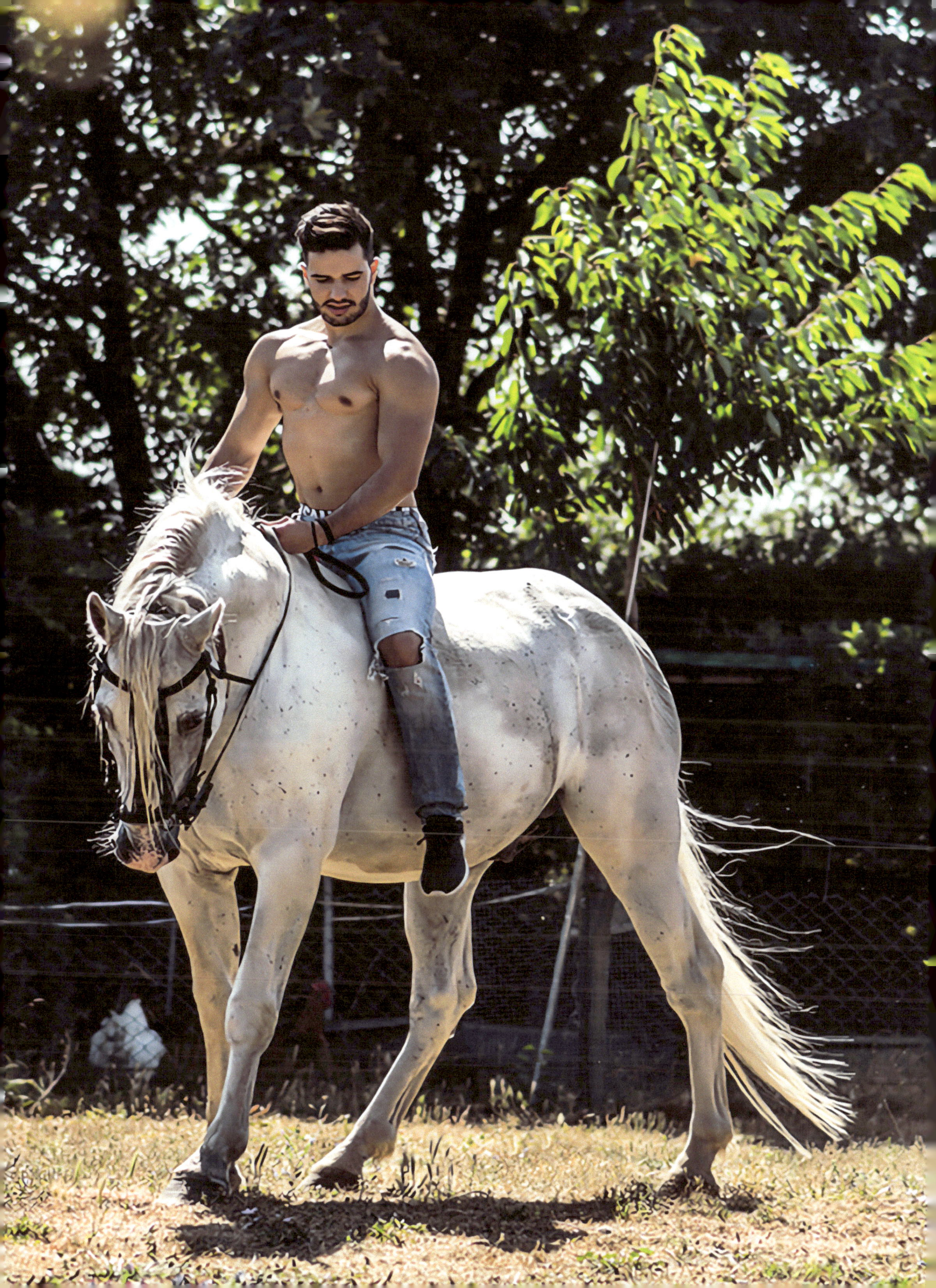

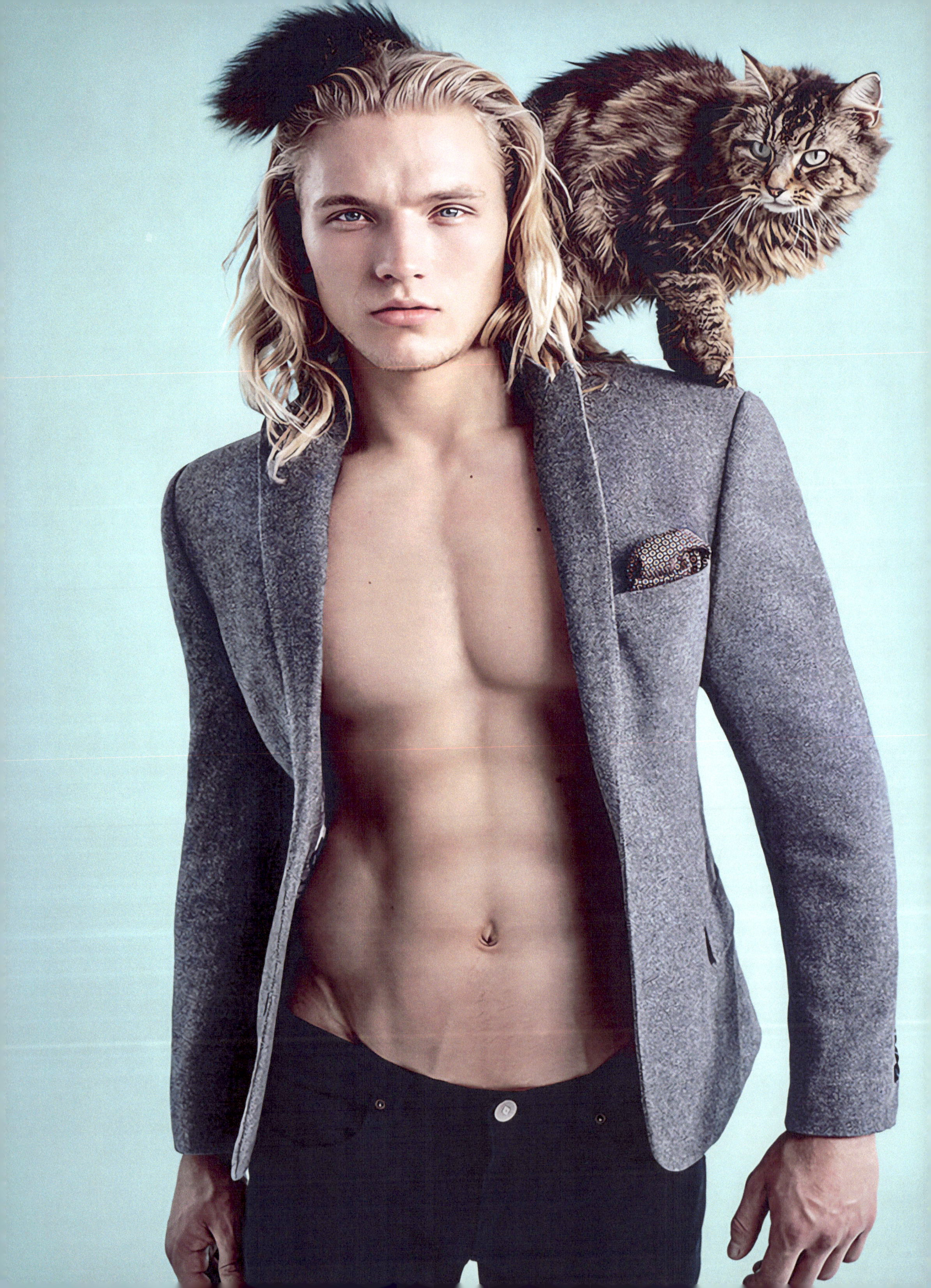

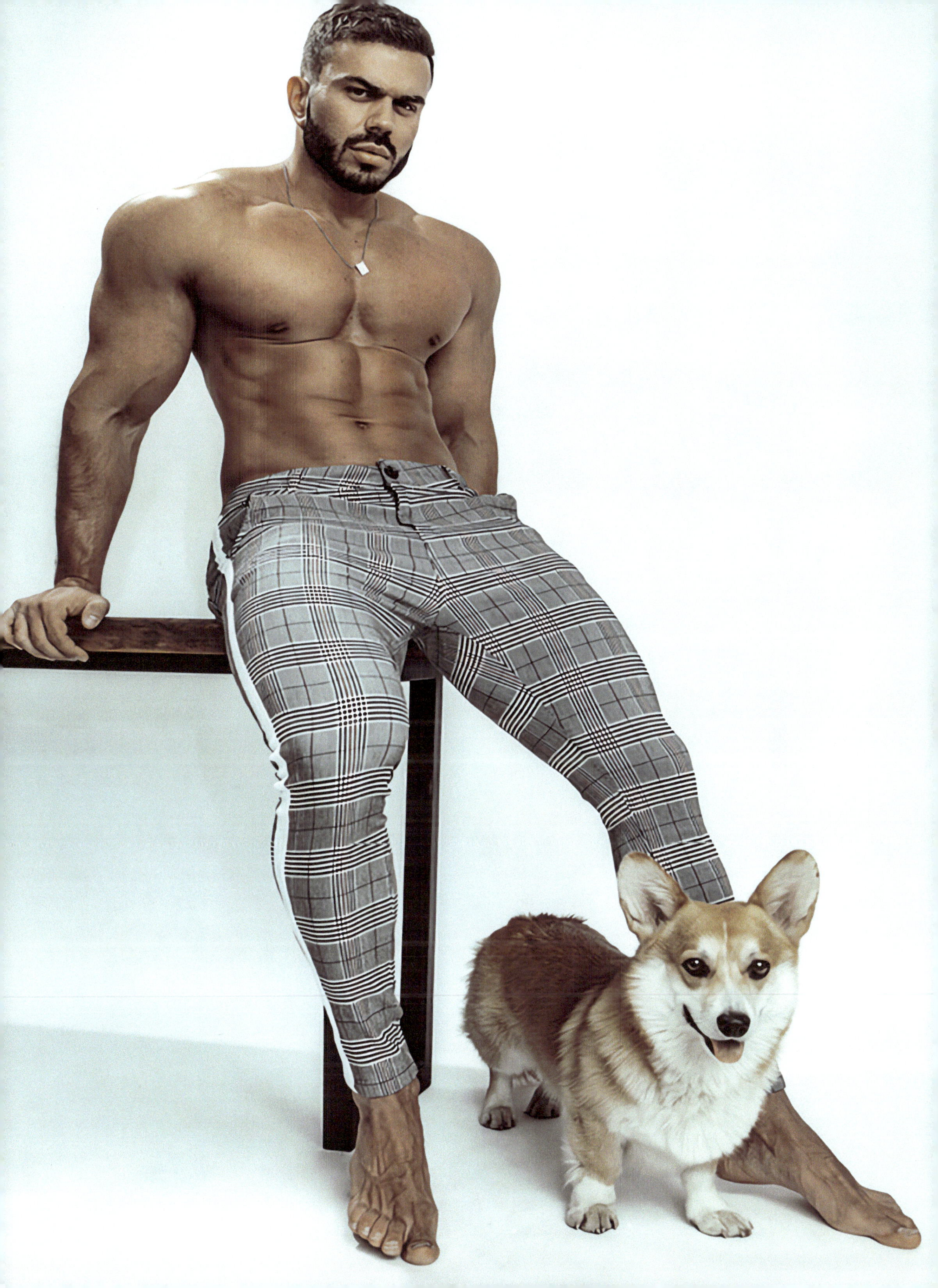

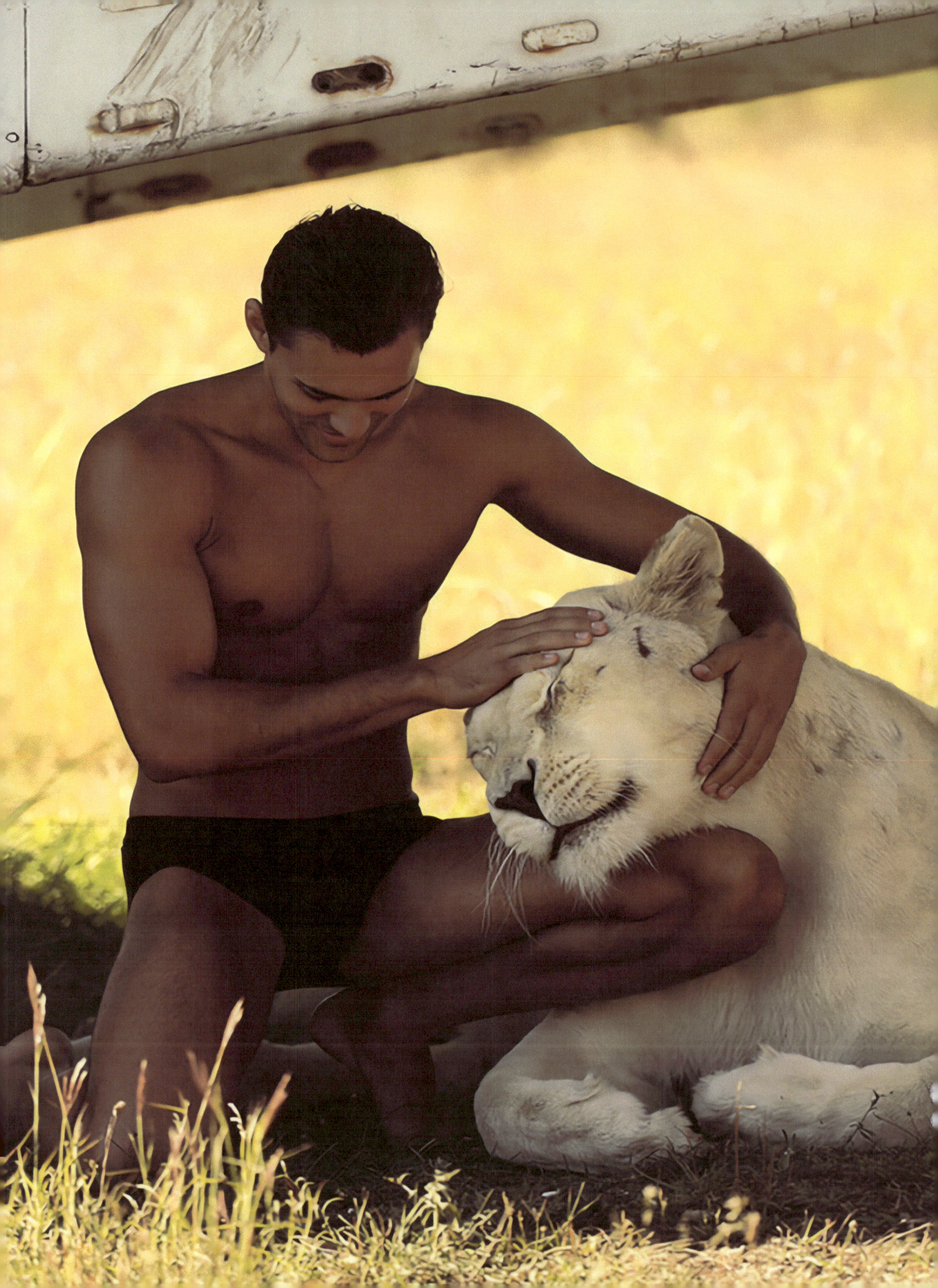

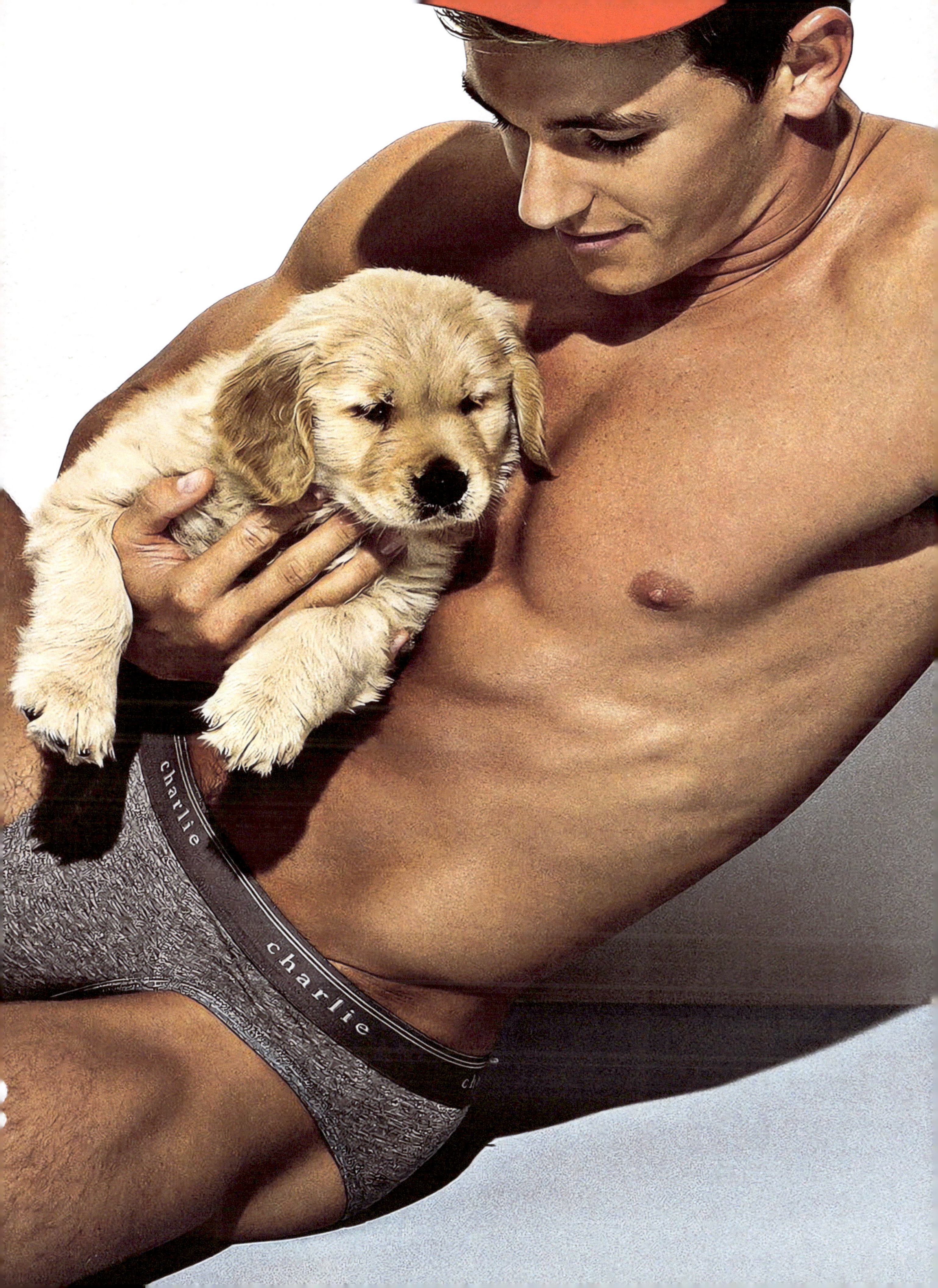
charlie
charlie

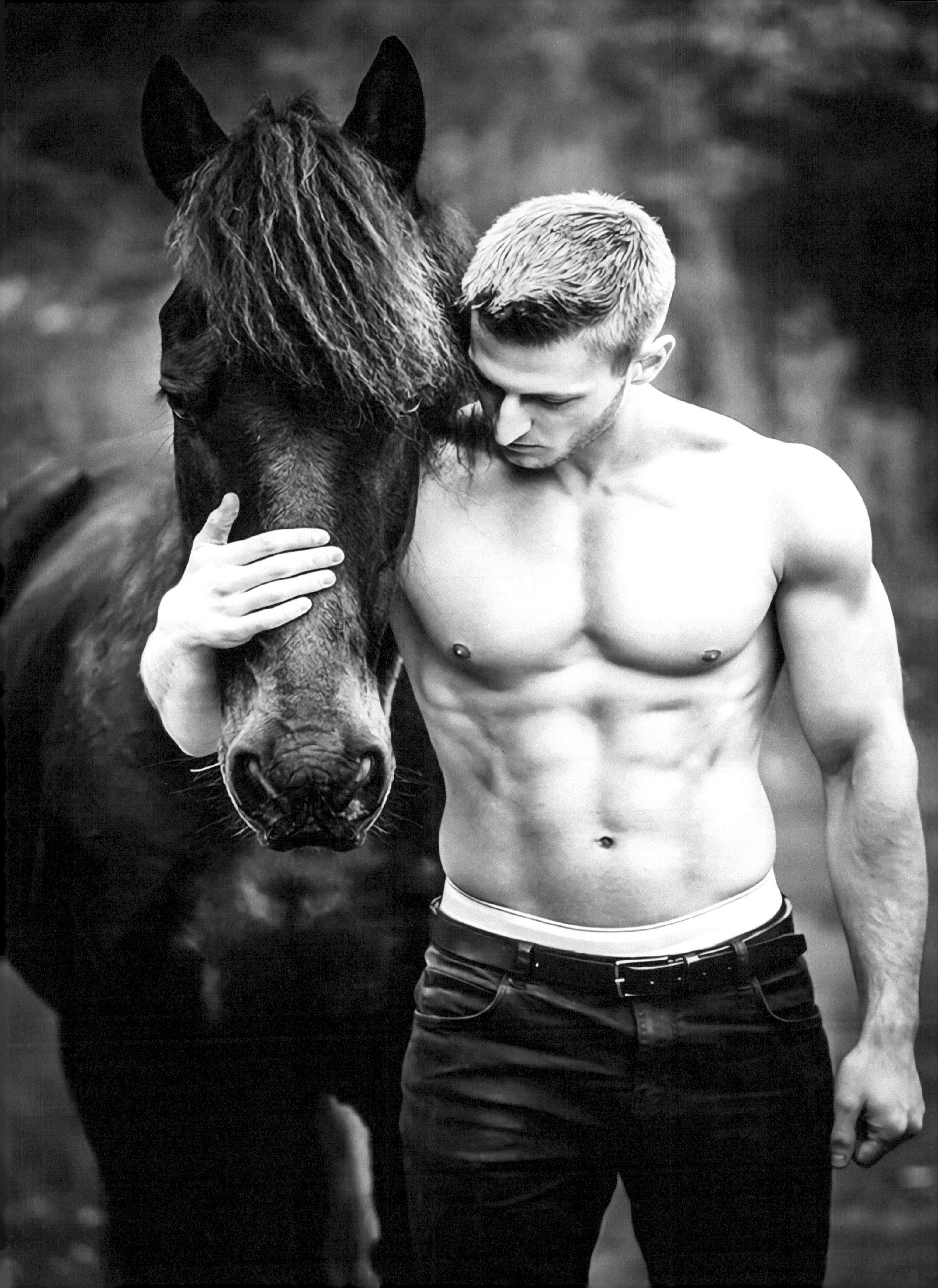

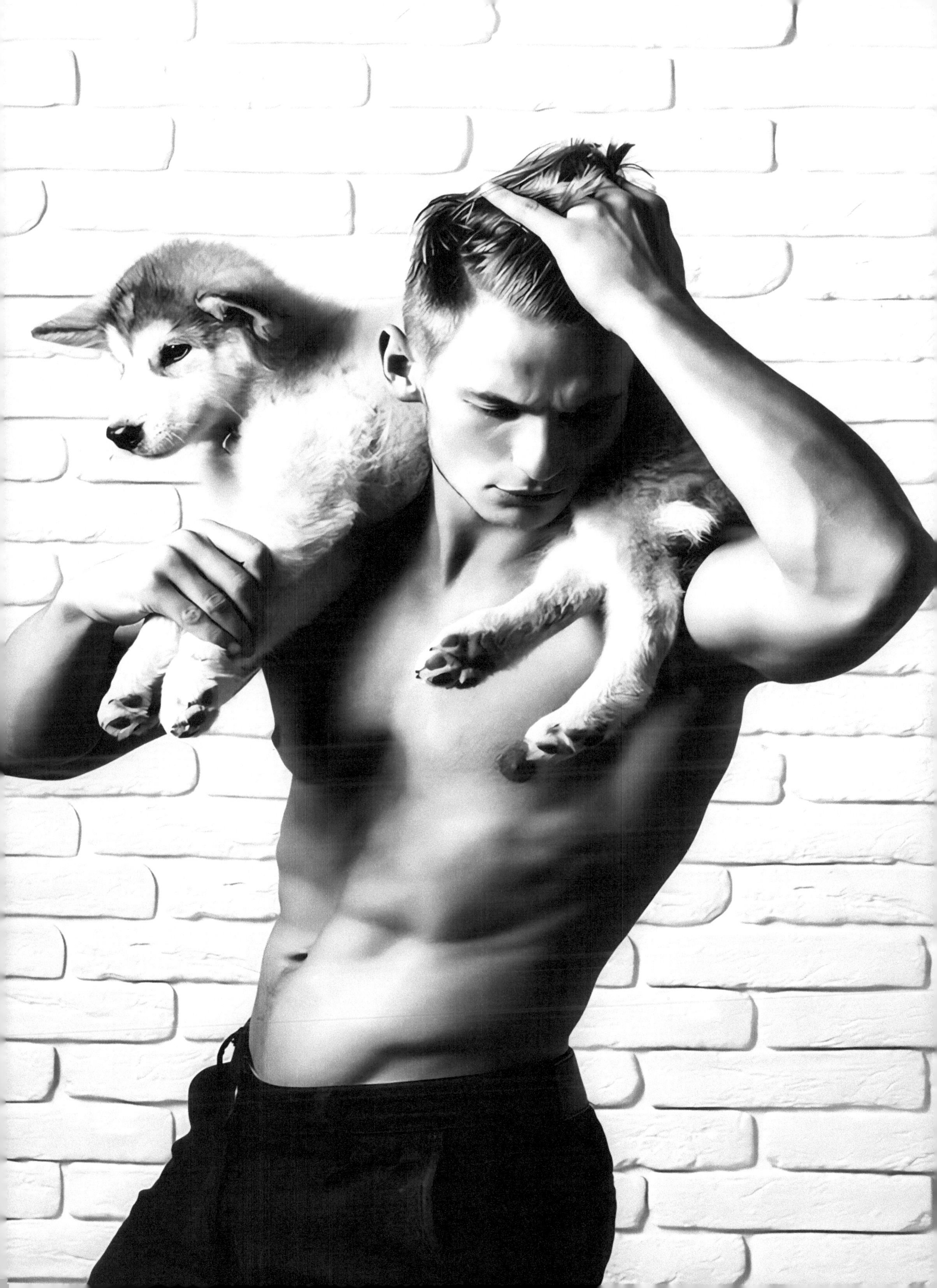

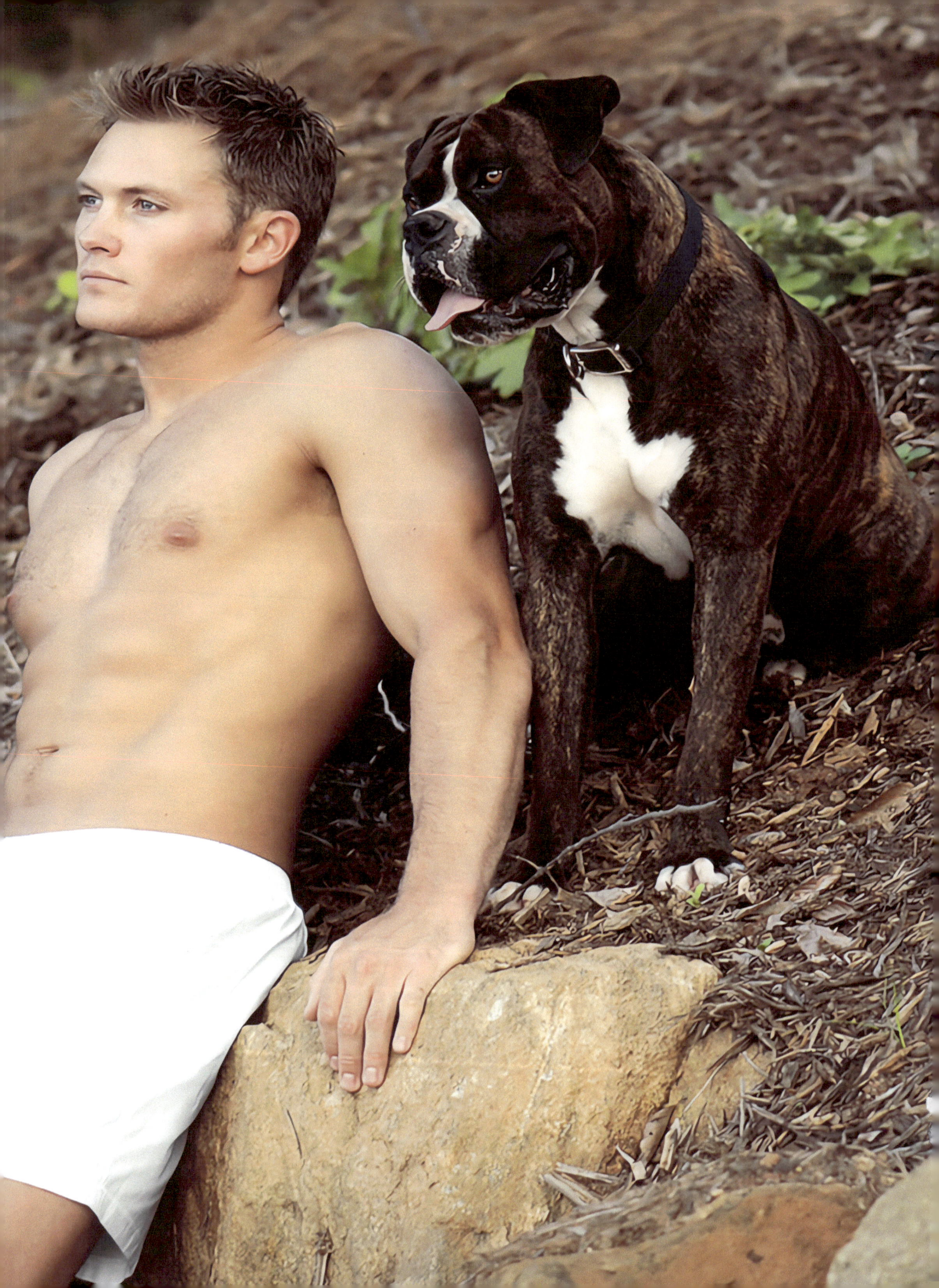

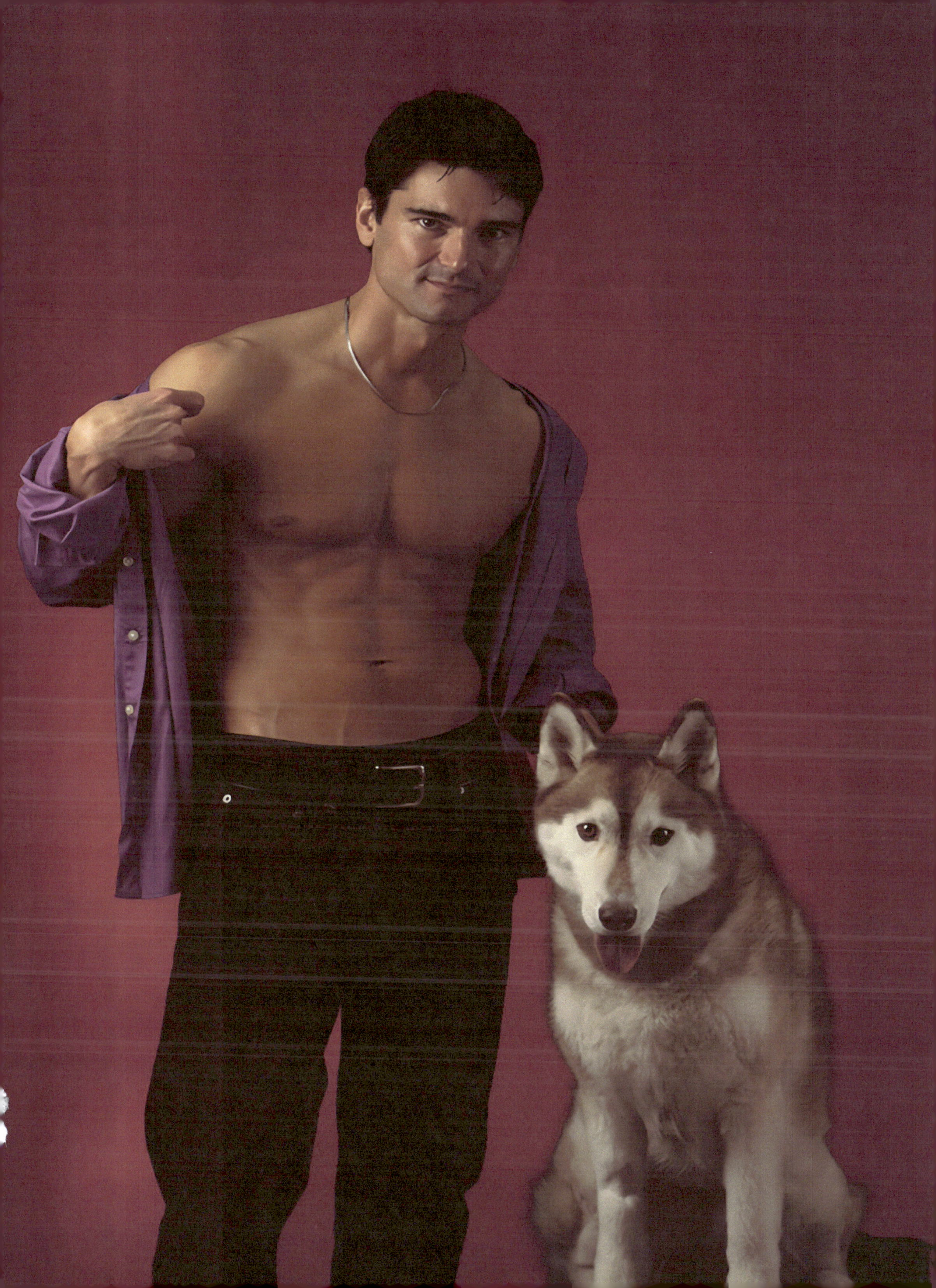

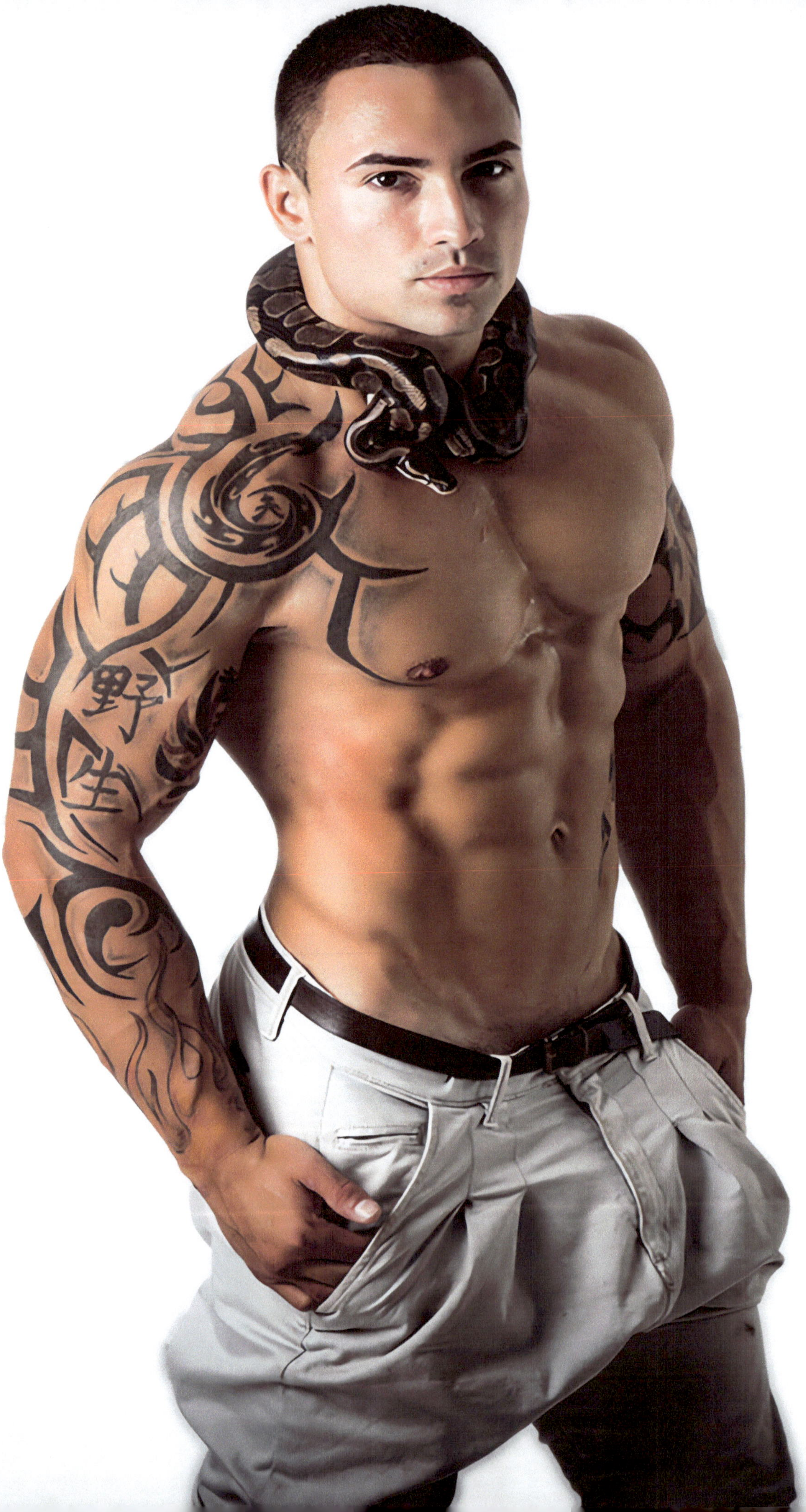
野生

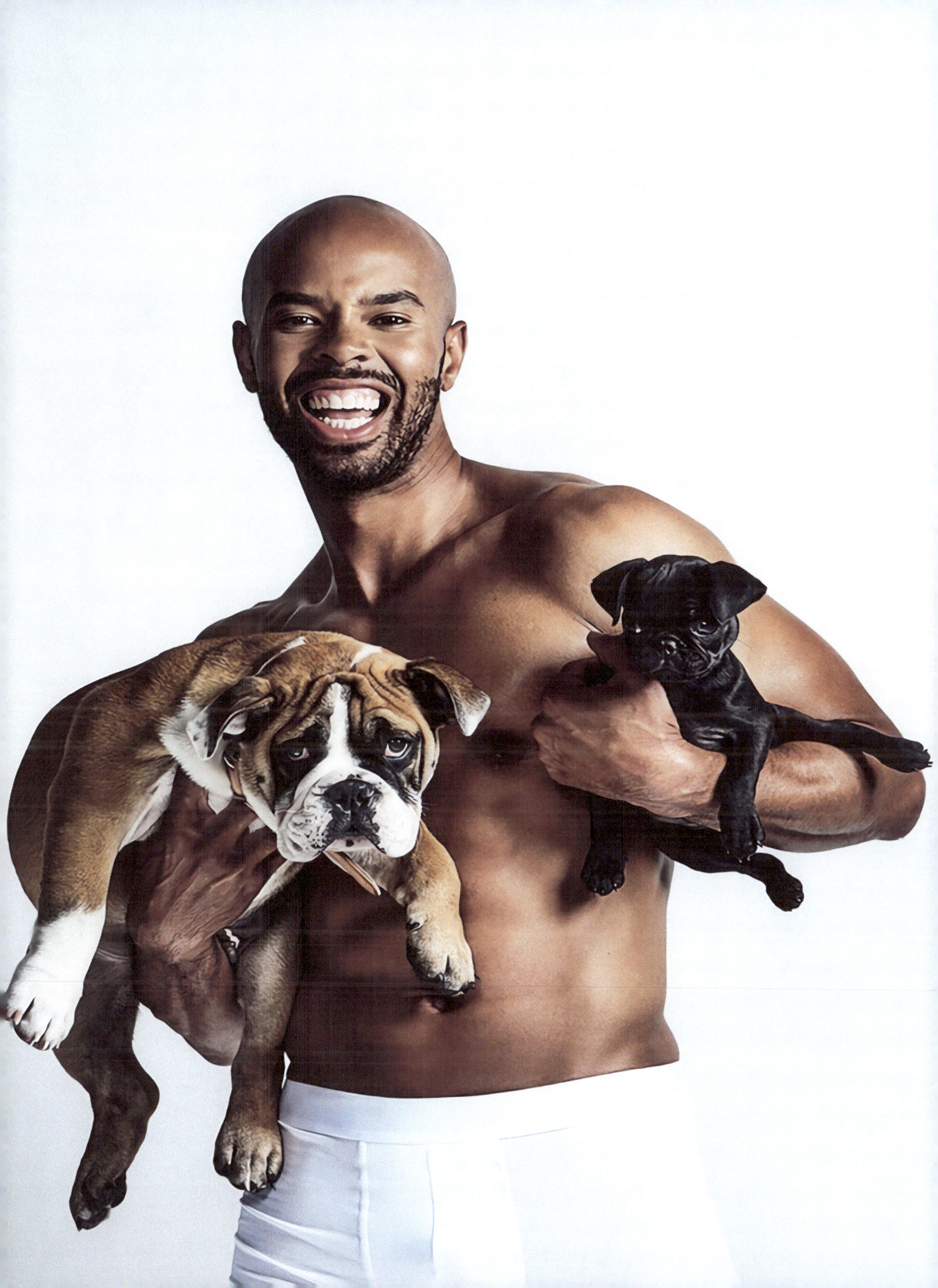

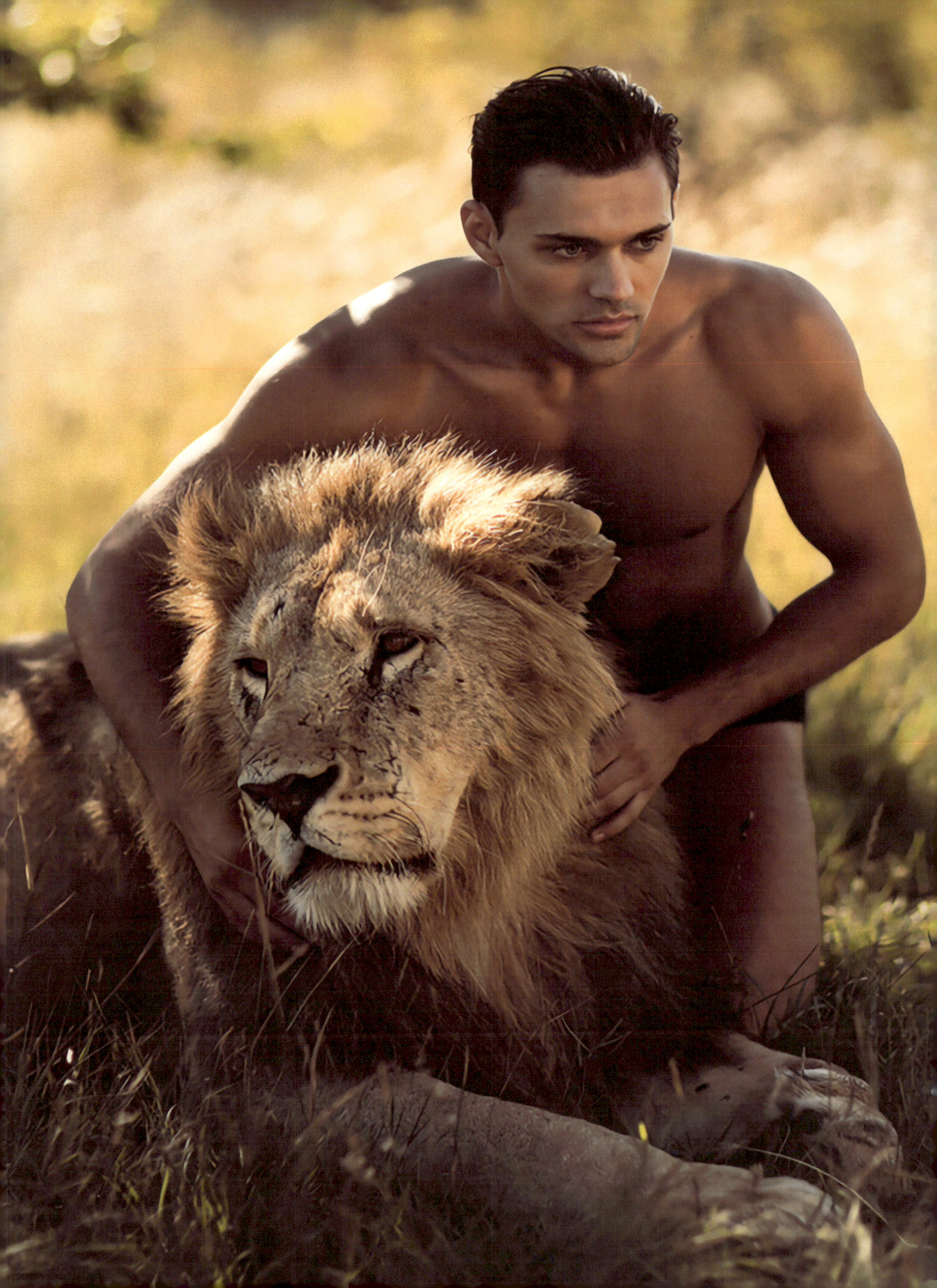

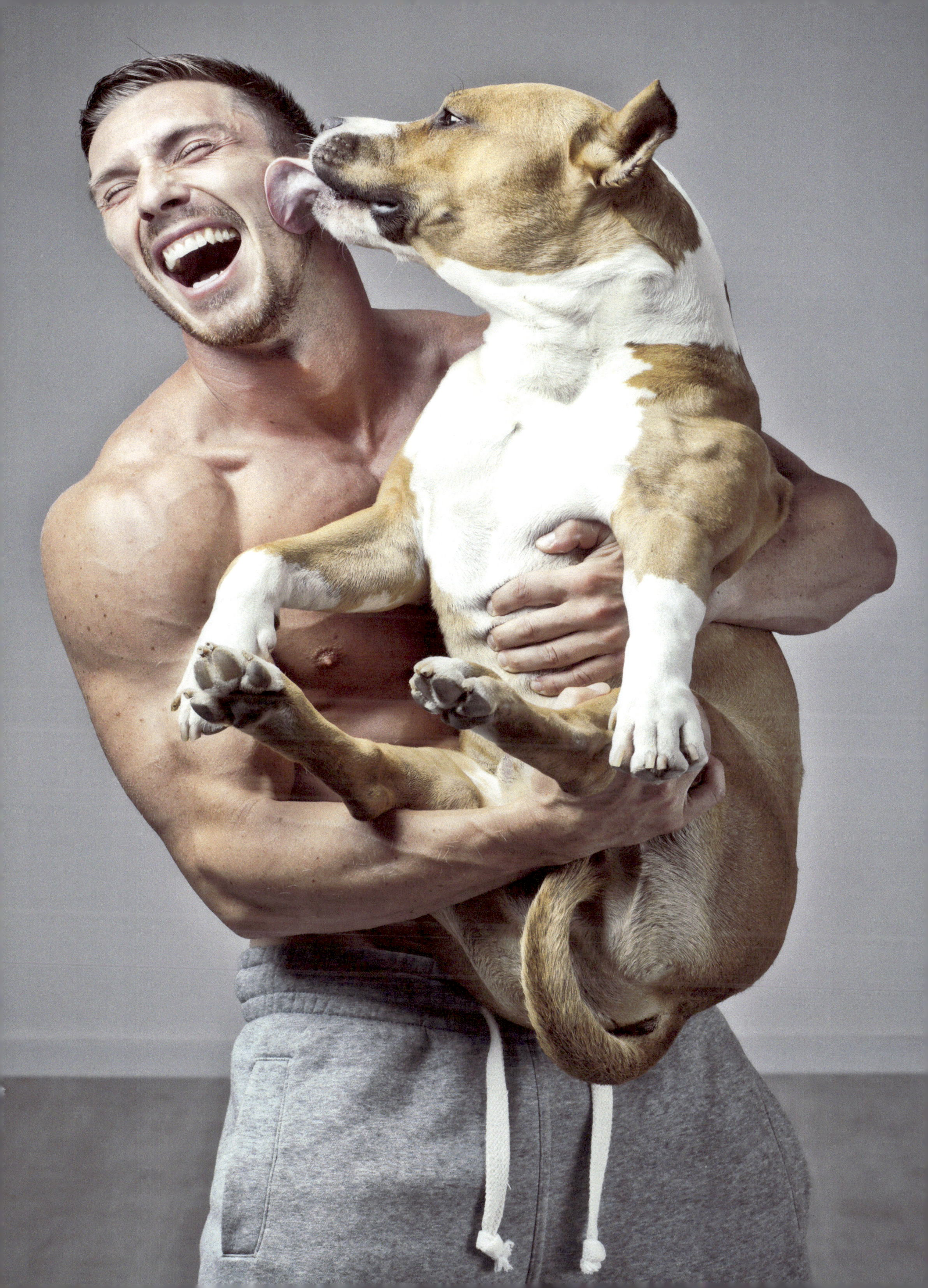

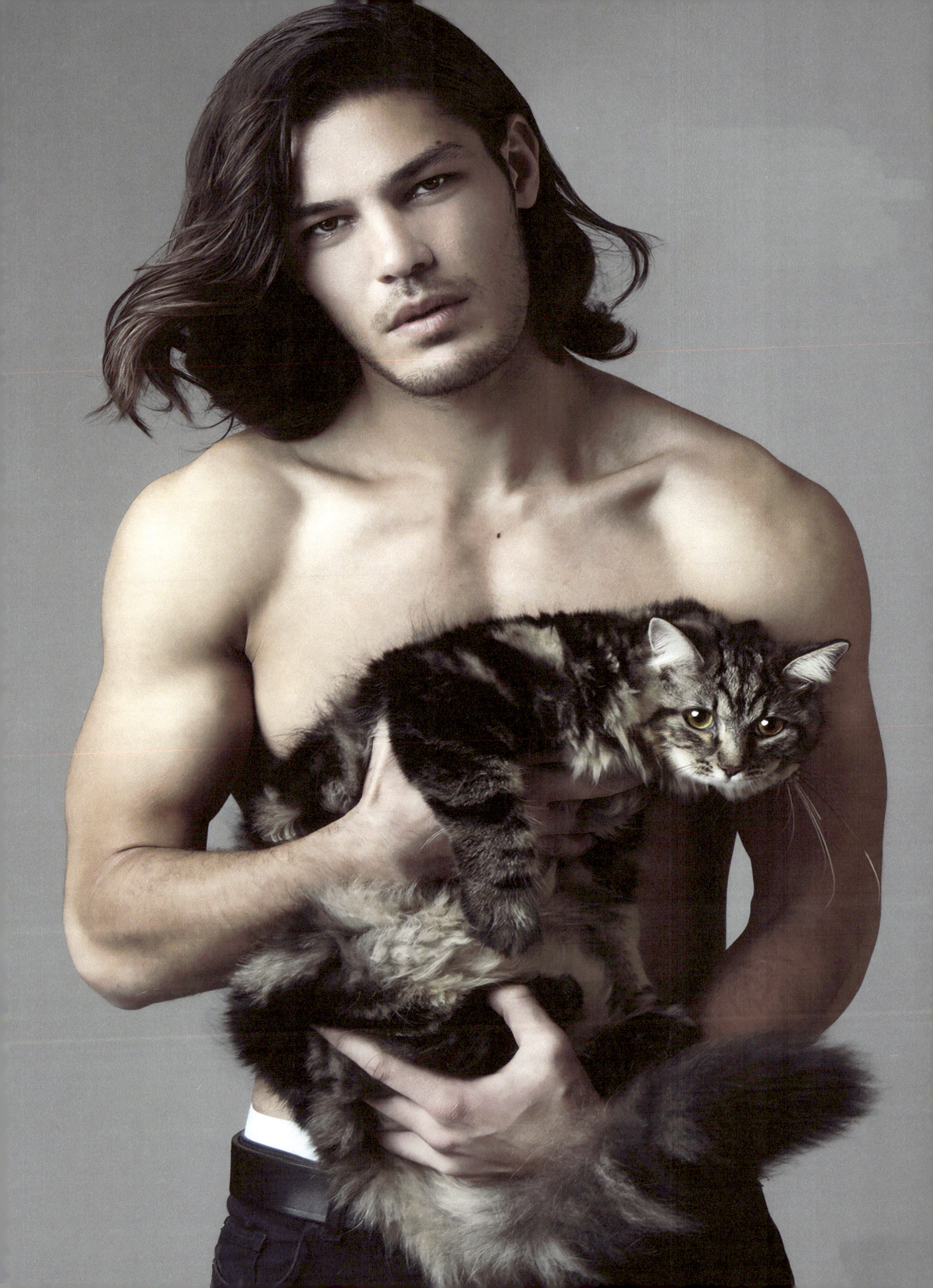

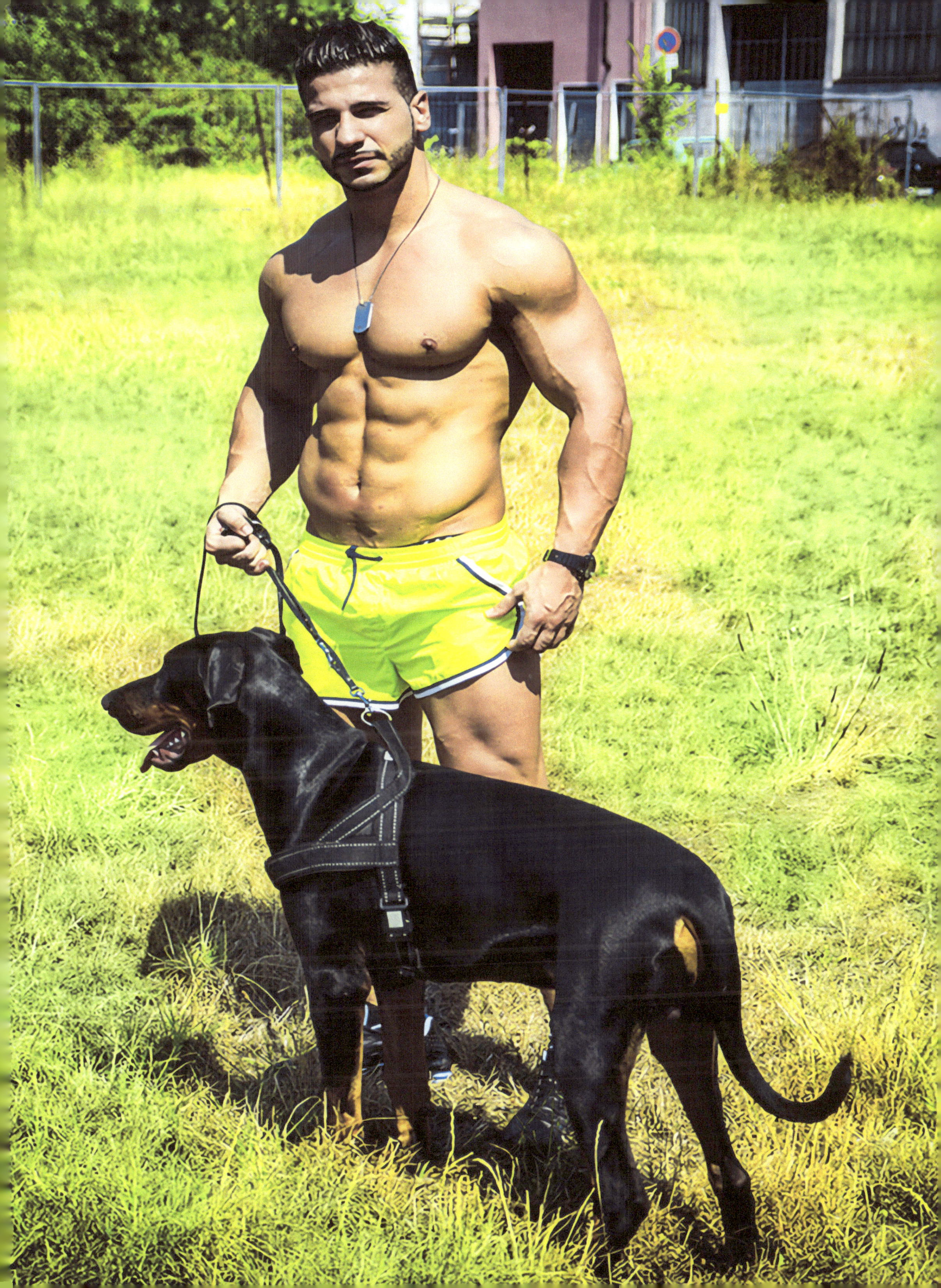

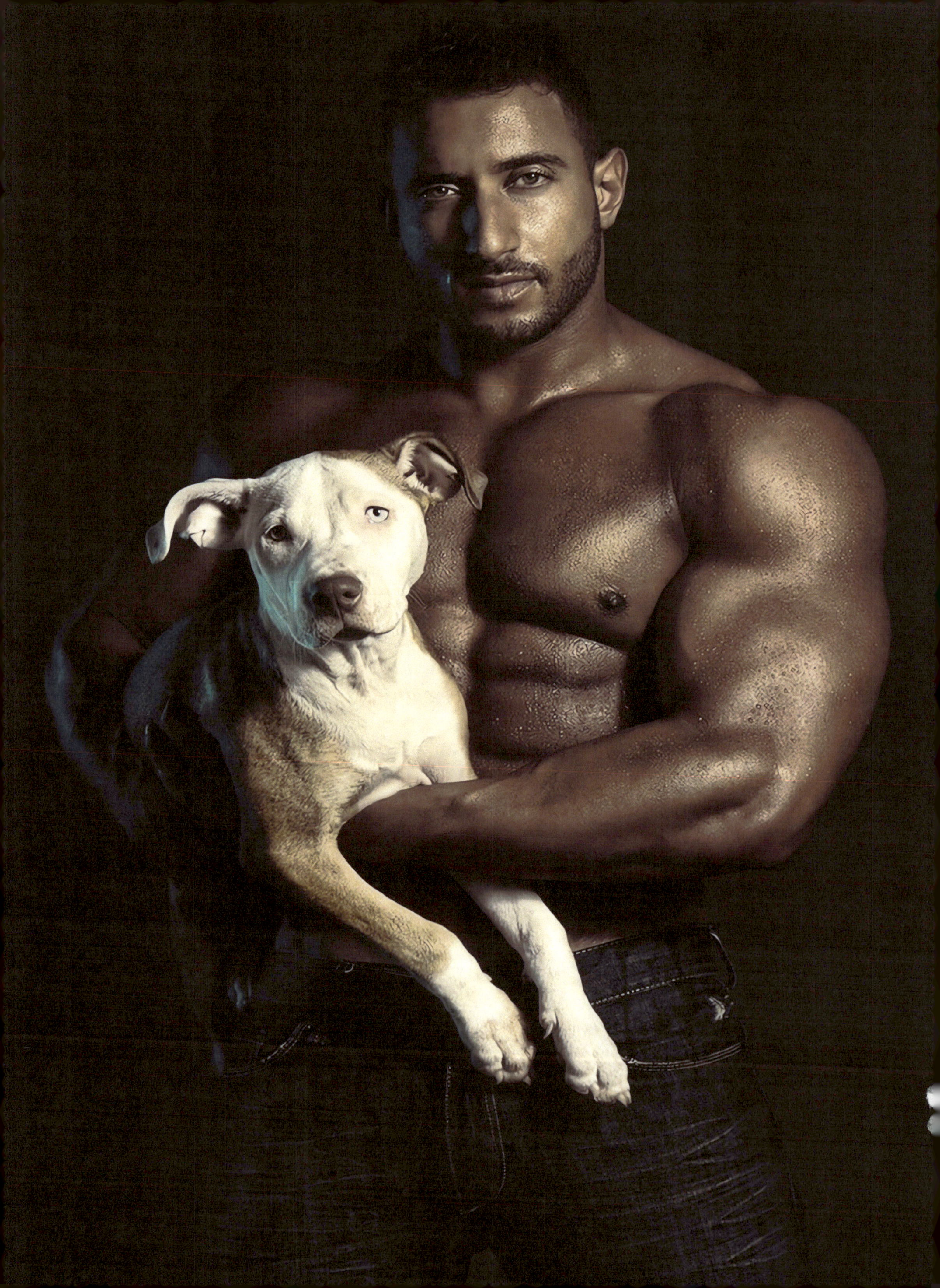

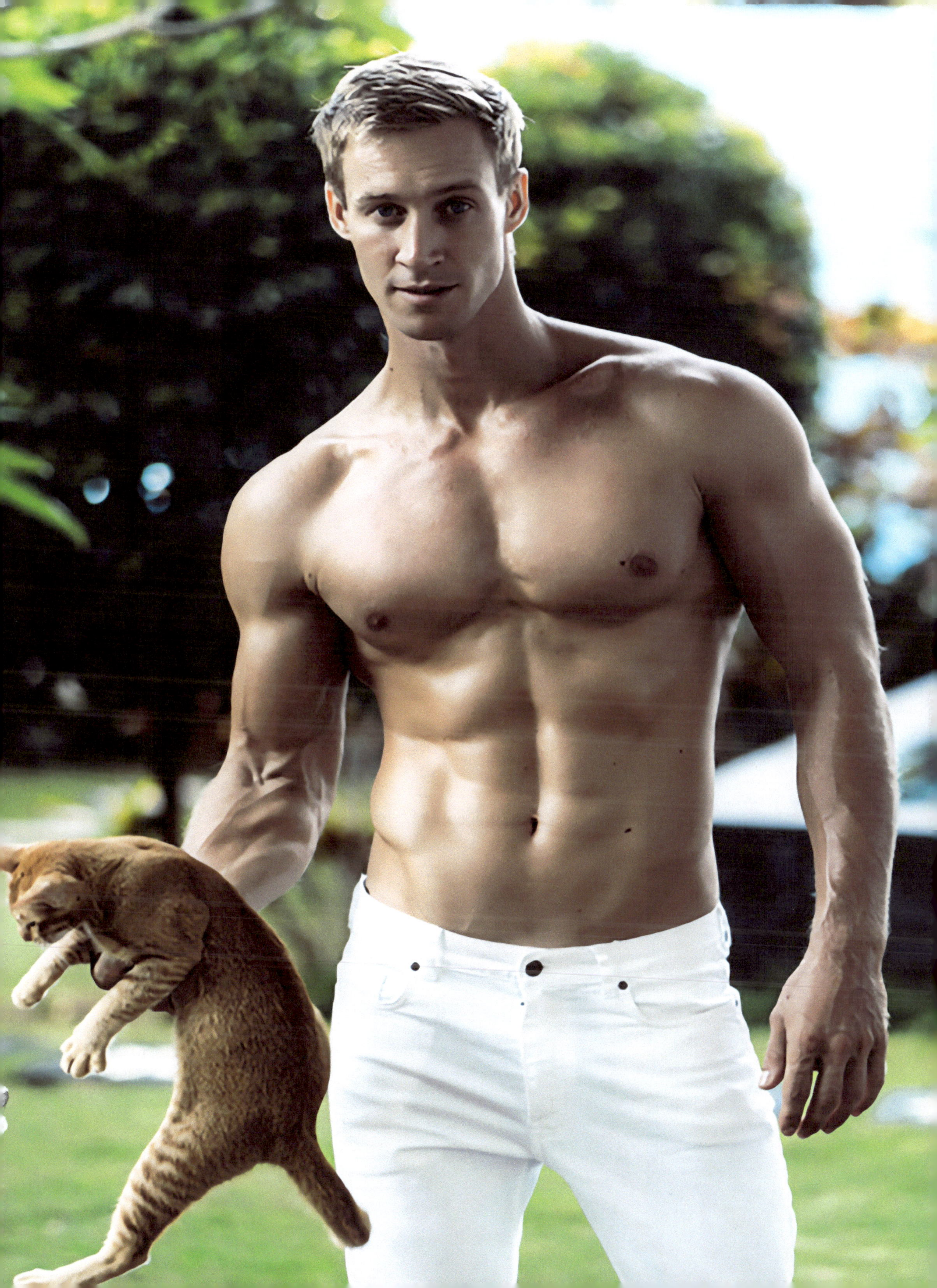

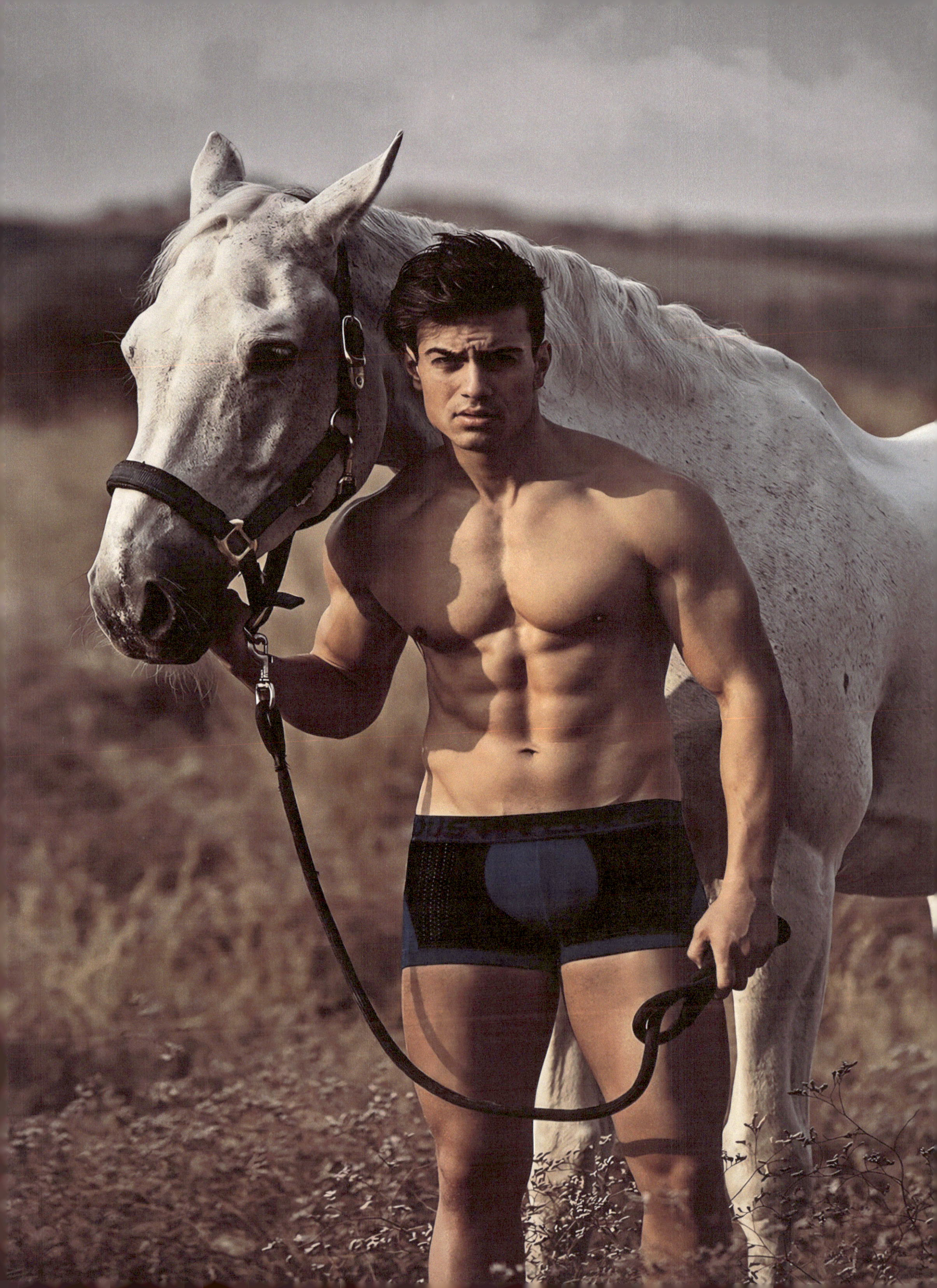

www.ingramcontent.com/pod-product-compliance
Lightning Source LLC
Chambersburg PA
CBHW051827210526
45473CB00005B/1771
9798303113930